To Candace
Blessings of
Clifton McKenzie

Push
Thru!

CleRenda McGrady

Moravia Street Publishing, LLC.
Los Angeles, CA

Dedication

This book is beyond a book. It is a movement. So therefore, this movement is dedicated to none other than my family.

To my mother, who smiles down on me from Heaven. Aloa JoAnn Harris was the epitome of everything good and right. I know perfect doesn't exist, but she was as close to perfect as possible. Her genuine sweet, giving and kind spirit, her love for people, her heart to serve, her unwavering love for her children, her many sacrifices and choices to go without in order for her family to have, her steadfast faith, belief and love for God and her character and integrity have all shaped who I am and the legacy that I will leave.

To my father who also smiles down from Heaven, who instilled strong work ethic, toughness, resilience and the wherewithal to rise back up after the fall. His art of storytelling taught me and allowed for the creativity of my own stories.

To my "Harris Clan"— Clevell, Candice, Christian, Cayla, CleAnn, Blake, Brenda, Jackie, Gwen — I love you and grateful for you.

To my four most incredible and treasured children, who are honestly the best kids ever. I love you, and because of you, I am a better me. Always know that you are chosen for greatness – the world needs you!

Layla — your wisdom beyond your years, intuitiveness, and character always amazes me and makes me proud!

Laymen — your inquisitiveness, kindness, and willpower makes me well-pleased!

Laycee — your sweet, loving and caring spirit makes me smile!

Layden — your fearlessness, strength, and determination inspires me!

To my beloved husband, Tracy — I love you. I adore you. You are my King and my everything. Thank you for your love, support and friendship. You make me better. May God allow us to forever "create our own success story."

To my God — thank you for choosing me, trusting me and appointing me. All praises and glory are yours.

Acknowledgements

Danielle Pollard, Nouveaux Dimensions — Thank you for always working with such class, spirit of excellence, and for reminding me that there is "no shortage of information." Thank you for your constant support and taking care of all my "simple" ideas, which has allowed me to focus on this book project.

Martin Gaston, Gaston Productions — Thank you for seeing that there was a "machine" and for being a part of making the machine work.

Diane Palmer, DP Marketing Strategies — Thank you for "seeing" the book before there was ever a book, for helping me to push this book out and for identifying and reminding me of "the pink elephant in the room."

DP Marketing Strategies Team — Thank you for all of your help and support.

Karla Thornhill Coleman — Thank you for going on the journey with me as my editor, making yourself available and helping me get to the finish line.

Renee Clark — Thank you for sharing your vision from your dream years ago that I would "have influence and impact amongst women."

Valorie Burton — Thank you for challenging, stretching and encouraging me!

Pat Williams — Thank you for believing in me, supporting me and for all of your many gifts to the world!

Elissa Grabow — It's been over 20 years with you. I'm grateful for all that you have been to my family and me. Much love to you and thank you.

Lisa Nakawatase — From back then, to now and always...love you girl!

Nicole West — You inspire me to Push Thru!

Tomeka Holyfield — You have always been so encouraging, believed in me and cheered me on! Thank you!

"Rey Rey," Chef Reynold Darthard — Thank you for your constant support and friendship!

To Tina Thomas, Angela James, Nikki Smith, Sylvia Ochier, Jenine Howard, Tasha Marbury and Denise Malloy — Thank you for true friendship and sisterhood. Your friendship has been a safe, loving and trusted refuge for me. I love you all. Tina and Nikki — Ya'll make me smile! Thank you for always having my back, for the laughs and the prayers! Denise Malloy — Thank you for always pushing me to be better, and to always see the "good" and the possibilities in people and in life. Jenine Howard — You have been there for me as I've pushed thru so much...in life, love and even birth. Love you. Tasha Marbury — From our days in Winston through the years and up to now — Together we've pushed thru on so many levels. Love you. Angela James — Thank you for being a steady rock and for showing me what *"Pushing Thru!"* looks like. Love you!

My brother, Clevell Harris, Harris Designs — Thank you for always being available for my graphics, artwork, design, and creativity with my projects. I love my book cover! You have been my "team" before there ever became a team. Thank you for your constant support and love. I love you.

Brendolyn — Thank you for filling in the gap and helping with your "grandbabies" so that I can create and produce. Love you!

To my sister, CleAnn — Thank you for always loving me and encouraging me (and for "making" me go to school and face "Monica Booker!"). I love you.

Cover by: Clevell Harris, Harris Design
Front cover photo by: Al Torres Photography
Make up by: India Henderson, CANVAS Makeup Artist
CleRenda McGrady is wearing a St. John boutique dress.

This book contains stories in which the author has changed some details in order to protect the privacy of others.

Published in association with the marketing agency of
DP Marketing Strategies, Inc. P.O. Box 3773 Southfield, MI 48076
www.dpmarketingstrategies.com

Push Thru!
Copyright © 2016 by CleRenda McGrady
Published by Moravia Street Publishing LLC.
1880 Century Park East, Los Angeles, CA 90067
www.clerendamcgrady.com

Library of Congress Cataloging in Publication Data
    McGrady, CleRenda 2016
    Push Thru! / CleRenda McGrady
ISBN 978-0-692-34052-3 (pbk)
ISBN 978-0-692-81121-4 (ebook)
1. Self Help--Success. Purpose. 2. Self Help--Motivation. Self Improvement.

All scripture quotations, unless otherwise indicated, are taken from The Holy Bible, New International Version.

What Do You Do With A Problem? By Kobi Yamada
Copyright © 2016 Compendium, Inc. Reprinted with permission.

Printed in the United States of America
10 9 8 7 6 5 4 3 2 1

Table of Contents

"Twenty years from now, you will be more disappointed by the things you didn't do than by the ones you did... sail away from the safe harbor."

Mark Twain

Foreword

I remember the moment I laid my eyes on CleRenda Harris for the very first time. She was beautiful, yes but there was something else about her. It was just the sense of goodness you felt when you were around her. I instantly got that sense she was kind-hearted and smart, very smart. I fell in love quickly and after dating for a few years I knew I wanted her to be my wife, my partner. I knew I had found the love of my life.

As my athletic career started to take off, our lives got crazy, yet she was the steady in my life. The years of playing professional basketball presented some of the most memorable and profound times in my life and some of the most painful ones too. CleRenda never wavered as we lived life inside the NBA with all its challenges. She remained right there by my side, always. She has been my compass and there isn't a day I am not in awe of this woman.

Seeing her raise our four incredible kids is like watching a woman literally able to do it all. She embodies the definition of a loving dedicated mother. She is faithful, soulful and I never truly know how she does it all. Her tank is never empty.

When she developed her non-profit Project P.U.S.H., I watched my wife find her passion and live her truth. As a professional athlete I got it. It was in her and it needed to come out. When she would talk about it, I could see how much joy it brought her. No matter how much time she dedicated to breathing life into her projects and this book, (and believe me, it took a lot of time and energy) her family always came first. The love she has for our family is the bedrock of who she is. She is the glue to our family and makes it all work. I am honored to share my life with such a strong and loving woman.

CleRenda has something incredible to share with the world and is making an impact by inspiring others to find their truth and to believe in their potential. At her first Project P.U.S.H. conference, I was listening to her speak from her heart and share stories that connected with other women. I was in the back of the room and watched as everyone in that room embraced her words as they found peace in her message. You saw it on their faces and the energy in that room could be felt. It was spiritual and it affected everyone in attendance.

The people who were inspired in that conference weren't the only ones that experienced something pretty special that day. My heart skipped a beat as I watched our two daughters, Layla and Laycee, sitting front row looking up at their strong and powerful mother, showing them the way. What a role model she is for so many. I couldn't be more proud of her. This book is not just for women, the fellas can learn a lot too. I promise you will benefit from her guidance and support. I do on a daily basis.

Tracy McGrady

Introduction

I have joyfully given birth to four babies, and with each child, I remember the anticipated excitement that led up to each of their arrivals. As the days drew closer – and I grew bigger – so many questions consumed my mind: "What will she or he look like? What will the labor and delivery be like? What will this time be like for me and my husband?"

Well, during the days leading up to the production of this book, I had very similar feelings of excitement – eagerly anticipating the arrival of yet another "baby." I am so proud that I've finally given birth once again. Not to a real, live baby, but a very live and real dream and purpose. This book is the product of one of my core messages — that we are "pregnant with purpose," but yet we often fail to go forth, push and give birth to the dream. It is my philosophy that before we're born, we're chosen and created to fulfill a certain purpose and assignment in life. When we fail to connect with and live in this God-given purpose, it creates an imbalance and an internal chaos that nags, tugs and pulls at us until we acknowledge it.

This book is my personal acknowledgment of those tugs, nudges and inner disturbances that have harassed me for years, until I decided to do something about it. I've been "pregnant" with so many dreams and desires, but for various reasons, I never gave birth. Now I'm embracing this wonderful season of life, where I am no longer choosing to play it small, but push beyond the obstacles that have kept me stuck and silent, and go after everything that I know was placed within me to do. As a motivator, life coach, speaker, author, wife and mother of four, my mission is simple – help women who are called to a bigger vision and version of themselves to push beyond the fear, insecurity and doubt that keeps them from rising to their full potential and purpose, so they can fulfill their dreams.

Push Thru! Redefine and Create Your Own Success Story is about overcoming the sabotaging and limiting beliefs that our success is attached to accolades, achievement and attainment. It inspires, encourages and empowers women, demonstrating that true success is connected to their purpose. Our success comes from being bold enough to reconsider and redefine how we view success. We are able to create our own success story without conforming to the pressures of the world by fitting in an existing mold. By sharing my personal stories, I hope you will be able to connect further with your purpose and define success based on YOU and no one else.

I pray that after reading this book you are encouraged to give birth to the dreams, visions and plans you were born to release. Is there something that for too long you have second guessed, told yourself it can't be done, downsized or made excuses why now isn't the time? Well, it's time for you to remember that dream, bring back that vision and know that you have been created, chosen and called for such a time as this – to walk fully in your destiny.

CléRenda

"If you think you can or you think you can't, your right!"

Henry Ford

chapter 1

birth of
a dream

CHAPTER 1:
Birth of a Dream

There I was – round as a beach ball, ripe as a peach, three days before my anticipated due date and wobbling around Orlando's Disney World theme park with Tasha, one of my closest friends. I noticed the stares and smiles from the other park goers, as if they wanted to say: "Shouldn't you be in a hospital somewhere instead of this park?" I smiled back in acknowledgment as I continued to eat my powdered funnel cake, sneak a bite from my friend's oversized turkey leg and search for the ride with the least wait time that could accommodate my "wide load."

Other than not being able to see anything below my enormous boobs and belly, and feeling a little like the Michelin Man, I felt totally fine and hadn't experienced any challenges – at that time or throughout my pregnancy. This was my first pregnancy and hanging out at Disney with my friend seemed to be a great way to get my mind off of my "any day now" status, get in a little exercise and have some fun.

All of a sudden, I felt a weird, slow, dripping sensation. For a moment, I had to question if I had an "accident" on myself. My friend asked if I thought my water had broken and perhaps we should leave the park. I assured her that it definitely wasn't my water – it couldn't have been. There was "no way" my water had broken (because according to the movies and documentaries I'd watched, it always looked like someone poured a bucket of water at the pregnant woman's feet). I didn't put much more thought into whatever was going on "down there."

I went on for another couple of hours with my friend, enjoying Disney World, as the slow drip continued. At this point in the pregnancy all kinds of changes were taking place. So, instead of listening to my friend's suggestion to leave the park and allow a medical professional to check things out, it was on to the next attraction. The next morning, I awoke to find that the dripping hadn't stopped during the night: I was now lying in a small puddle of fluid.

Needless to say, I was a little more concerned about the situation and wasn't as blasé as I was the prior evening at Disney. I quickly called my doctor and met him at the hospital. After an examination, he determined that indeed my water had broken the previous evening. The doctor, along with the nurses, immediately reprimanded me: I had put the baby and myself at risk by waiting almost 24 hours after my water had broken to come to the hospital! They would have to induce labor to deliver the baby as quickly as possible and reduce any further chances of infection or trauma.

Pushing From the Right Place

*S*ome hours later, on the birthing bed with a baby who was attempting to make her anticipated arrival, I was stuck. Frustration and exhaustion engulfed me because I knew my baby was "right there" on the brink of making her grand entrance, but not coming out. Sensing my frustration, my doctor calmly said, "CleRenda, your baby is right here. She is crowning and ready to come out. All you have to do is just push."

Considering that I was the one on the table – exhausted, worn out, sweaty and tired. Considering the pain was even more intensified because my labor was being induced, (coupled with no epidural anesthesia or any pain medication) I was a bit offended that this male doctor would have the nerve, the audacity, to suggest that all I had to do is "just push!" What in the world did he think I was doing: texting or checking social media or something? In a testy and snarly tone, I gritted my teeth and responded: "I AMMMM PUSHING!" He replied calmly back to me, "Yes, CleRenda, but you aren't pushing from the right place." He continued, "If you want your baby girl to come out now, you need to push from back here (as he tapped my bottom to indicate that dreaded place where in actuality I should have been pushing from) and not there."

I heard what my doctor said, and understood very clearly the place where he said to push from. Although I was in the middle of giving birth and had silenced almost every other thought from my mind in order to focus, I still had my good sense and my dignity. I knew that if I pushed from "the place" that the doctor told me to push from, my baby girl wouldn't be the only thing that I'd possibly "push out." I would be putting myself in a very awkward, vulnerable, risky and possibly embarrassing position on that delivery bed, right there in front of the doctor, the nurses and most importantly, my husband!

No way was I going to put myself in a situation where my husband would forever carry the visual of me pooping on myself. As much pain as I was in and as much as I wanted that child out of my body and into this world, I couldn't help but worry if I would do a "number two" on that delivery table if I pushed from "the place" my doctor was telling me to push from. Even in my distress, I wasn't going to be fooled. I had seen all the talk shows and other TV specials, where husbands confessed that after watching their babies birthed, along with "other bodily excess," it was difficult to continue to view the image of their wives as desirable. Yes, the most fascinating, miraculous and beautiful event in life and nature, turned into one that scarred those men for quite some time. Oh no! That was not going to be my story!

I know, I know! You must be thinking: how vain, self-centered, pretentious and non-maternal of me to be focusing on something as insignificant and superficial as using the bathroom on myself and what my husband would think, instead of focusing on the blessing, miracle and beauty of God's creation taking place at that very moment. Perhaps that has never been a concern to any of you that have delivered a child, but at that split moment, as a first-time mommy, it most certainly crossed my mind.

So, as I lie there taking in everything the doctor had just instructed me to do and weighing it against all the other thoughts that were consuming my mind in that short amount of time, I decided not to listen to his orders: I would continue to push my way. Although it wasn't very effective, and I wasn't getting the results I wanted, my way seemed to be the safest and it sure beat his way, which was risky, leaving me in a vulnerable, open and possibly embarrassing situation. So I did just that and continued pushing my way, from the place that in reality, wasn't getting me anywhere, except more tired, frustrated, exhausted, worn out and burned out.

After what appeared to be an eternity, which in reality was just a couple more failed attempts at pushing, I did what we all do when we get tired of banging our heads against the wall and getting nowhere. In all my pain and anguish, I cried out: "OK!" My doctor, ever so patiently, looked back up at me as though he knew what I had been contemplating, and said, "She is right here, your baby is ready to come out. All you have to do is push from the right place. Are you ready?" And you better believe that by the time the next labor pain hit me, I quickly got over the prior internal dilemma of the embarrassment of possibly "pottying" on myself, and I finally chose to push from the "right place."

Now before you look back at the book cover in confusion to make sure you didn't pick up a pregnancy and delivery book, stay with me here. Once I got over my fear of embarrassment and the unknown and changed my thought process, followed the doctor's orders and did it his way – the right way – I was able to give birth to my beautiful and perfect baby girl, Layla.

That day, I learned a very valuable life lesson on the birthing table, which is applicable to success in everyday life. Oftentimes in life, we find ourselves "pregnant with purpose." We are pregnant with dreams, visions, plans and ideas that we carry around, but yet fail to give birth to them – all because we are pushing from the wrong place. These "wrong places" are often places of fear, insecurity, doubt, rejection, guilt, shame, past disappointments, and unproductive or toxic relationships. Because we push from the wrong places in life, and although we may end up giving birth, it's often to a downsized, smaller version and fraction of the size dream that was originally placed within us. And just as often, because we abandon pushing altogether, our dreams, visions, plans and ideas are left aborted.

The biggest thing that held me back on that delivery table was fear. The fear of embarrassment and of what could have potentially happened, stopped me from pushing the way I was instructed too. How many times does thoughts of rejection and disapproval from others hold us hostage and keep us from birthing those things that we want most?

LIVING AND LEARNING

he lessons I learned on the birthing table are the foundation for the rest of this book. In a short amount of time on that birthing table, I learned that I had to change how I was thinking, which then allowed me to change what I was producing. In other words, once I changed my thoughts, I changed my actions. I changed what was keeping me stuck, stagnate and circling. I could no longer operate from a place of fear of the unknown. To get what I needed and desired, I made a decision to be vulnerable, to take a risk, to make a mess, to do the uncomfortable, to listen to the authority, to go beyond my comfort zone and push like never before.

And speaking of listening to authority, the lessons on the birthing table reminds me that often there is a form of authority already set in motion that we sometimes chose to ignore. My doctor, who was instructing me as to the proper way to give birth was my authority. I chose not to listen. We have these same authority figures set before us that guide, instruct, teach and correct us that we may choose to ignore as well. This can be people who have gone before you or the spiritual authority that governs your life. Whatever that authority is, when we are not in alignment, get off track and attempt to do things out of order, we find ourselves inviting in more confusion and chaos and experience a longer and more intense labor.

By keeping the beauty and blessing of the end result of what I desired in mind, I was able to shift my thoughts and change what wasn't working in order to push through. And how apropos to life as we know and live. How often do we choose to take the more comfortable and convenient, safe and familiar, easy and acceptable route, instead of the best one? The best routes are usually not the sexiest, most popular or painless.

However, whether it is a baby or a dream, there is nothing easy, comfortable, sexy or pain-free about giving birth. Perhaps you are pregnant with a dream that you yearn to accomplish. If so, you are carrying around a wonderful divine gift to the world. Your "baby" is ready to make its grand entrance. Surely you have felt the nudge, the tug and the labor pains and now it is your time. It's time to give birth, to deliver that really "big thing" that you've thought about and carried around inside for way too long. We can't continue to stay in our comfort zones, afraid of the greatness that lies within and ahead. It is your birthright to live a life of boldness and confidence and to manifest the plan and desires of your heart.

One of my favorite passages is a great reminder that we are in a birthing season. Jeremiah 29:11 states: "For I know the plans I have for you...plans to prosper you, not to harm you. To give you hope and a future." It's time to step into that plan, be confident in that hope and say yes to the future that is already yours. And if you are or have been anything like me, then you too are in or have experienced a season of life where you felt stuck, stagnate, frustrated and not experiencing the breakthrough that you desire. Perhaps you have been pushing, but unfortunately, since you have been pushing from the wrong place(s), you have not given birth to the incredible divine dream that impregnates you trapped within and so desperately seeking to come out.

Along my journey of life, I couldn't have given birth without "midwives." Pregnancy is hard. And in order to give birth to something great, you need midwives to walk along side of you, to journey with you and to help you push and give birth to your dream. I have had many midwives; some don't even know they have been a part of my midwife tribe. Some I have actually never even met and they don't even know that I exist – they're people I have admired and watched from afar. Some of my midwives have been family members, friends, mentors, teachers, pastors, church leaders, public figures and even to a degree, strangers. Anyone that has helped shape me, mold me, stretch me and grow me, I consider a part of my midwife tribe.

During the birthing season that you are in, you have to align yourself with midwives. You can't do this alone, at least not at the level that you are capable of and have the potential to produce. You can't afford to be around people who are draining, takers, whiners, criticizers and dream killers. The people you align yourself with are critical components of your success. Surround yourself with people who support you, get you, encourage you and see in you what you may not see in yourself. People that can pour into you and pray with you, for you and over you; people that show up for you, inspire you, motivate you, teach you, build you up and ignite you. Our midwife tribe must include those that can correct us, challenge us, constructively criticize us and aren't afraid to steer us back on track when we veer off. You must align yourself with people who are not afraid of holding you accountable. Part of our growth is being able to be challenged, even when it makes us uncomfortable.

Your God-given vision, dream, plan, message, desire, and "one day I want to" is right here, right now and ready to be birthed. You can't afford to not give birth to the dream. The world can't afford to go another day without it. Perhaps you have been like me, scared to push it out, fearful of how it will look and doubtful that it will be good enough. Whatever "it" is, the dream you have created, and are carrying around, has to be delivered. The dream and vision must come forth. Your destiny depends on it. Your "one-day, I'll do that" has expired. Today is that day. You can do this. You will do this. Prepare yourself for a delivery. It's time to give birth. It's time to *Push Thru!*

Ask Yourself...

- What are you "pregnant" with? What are the dreams and desires inside of you that you have yet to fulfill?

- What has kept you from executing or birthing your dream?

- How has "pushing from the wrong place" kept you stuck from birthing a dream?

- Who have you identified to be a part of your "midwife tribe?" The people that encourage you, inspire you and believe in you?

- During this season of birthing your dreams, who do you possibly need to consider disconnecting with? Which people are taking away instead of pouring into you?

"Be yourself and not anyone else."

--*Laycee McGrady, age 7*

chapter2

turning 40

CHAPTER 2:
Turning 40

I was totally fine with the idea of turning forty. I had so many people ask: how do you feel about turning forty this year? I would shrug my shoulders and respond, "I'm fine; I'm good." And I was. I didn't really get caught up in the whole mumbo jumbo rhetoric of turning forty until about four months out, when my husband started planning for my birthday party. Then, suddenly, it hit me. Remember that forty-year-old lady that twenty years ago I thought was so ancient: I'm about to be her!

I never thought sending out invitations to a birthday party could stir up so much turmoil and conversation. I guess certain people just didn't know I was even close to forty, and I was flattered that they thought I was a little younger. Remarks such as, "I thought you were in your early thirties" and "I thought you were closer to my age" became an ongoing theme.

I didn't think much about this milestone until people started responding to the invitation – calling, texting and e-mailing – flabbergasted by the "news." "I got your invitation. You're turning forty? Really? No way!" I thought, "Yeah, what of it? I'm turning forty, not a hundred." I actually had one friend tell me she opened up my e-invite to my birthday party at midnight and when she saw it, in disbelief, she woke up her husband. "Larry, did you know CleRenda is turning forty?" As she retells the conversation with her husband, I'm just trying to keep a smile on my face. But inside I am thinking: "Is it that big of a deal that you had to wake up your husband at midnight out of his peaceful sleep just to announce the news to him that I'm turning forty?"

With all the commotion and conversation that my birthday invite garnered amongst people, all centered around the newsflash of my age, what I thought was supposed to be a compliment, felt more like an insult. I started to think for a moment, "Oh my goodness, am I the only person in the world turning forty? Has no one else in life ever turned 40?" I know historically the big 4-0 always has been a big milestone to be celebrated. But it wasn't feeling like a celebratory occasion. This onslaught of disbelief began to do something to me. All of the "OMG, you're turning forty" comments started to rekindle insecurity and questions within my core. I had to have a moment of silence, block out all of the comments, and ask myself, what does turning 40 mean? Why has it always been a big milestone for people and what's really the big deal? So for me, when I began to think of what 40 should look like and feel like, I didn't fit the profile.

I started questioning my life leading up to this glory year. As I began to really think about what 40 "should" look like in the general population, one word popped into my head – success. By age 40, there should be some things accomplished, some bucket list items scratched off, and some empty boxes checked. By age 40, you should have "something to show for it" and be successful. By age 40, all of those things you once dreamed about, or what others dreamed for you, and what you thought you would have accomplished or acquired, well, by that point in life, you should have it all, right?

Well, if that's what turning 40 is "supposed" to look like, if that's what being successful is all about, it was time for me to reevaluate my life up to this point. And this is when I began to shift my thinking.

My Personal Breakthrough

*O*n paper my life on the edge of forty looked great. According to most people, the definition of success includes college degrees, a loving and accomplished husband that provides for his family, healthy children, a nice home, a nice savings, cool vacations, wonderful experiences and an all-around comfortable and "good" life. Check mark! Sounds "successful" to me.

With that kind of resume and checked off boxes, many people would say nothing is lacking and there should be nothing to complain or gripe about.

My complaining and griping wasn't anything audible and it wasn't about anything tangible. The gripe was more about an unsettled, incomplete feeling that had suddenly taken over my life. I felt a void of discontent: I was plagued by the thought that something was missing. I wasn't satisfied with myself or even how things looked on paper. What was this all about? It was not so long ago that I was totally fine with turning the big 4-0. Now I'm questioning my life up to this point and second guessing myself. But after much thought, reflection and prayer, my insecurities and questioning of myself had nothing to do with all of the chitter chatter of my rising milestone. No, these insecurities had obviously already been there, had already taken root and were very present – I just didn't realize it. These feelings of insecurity, fear and doubt were lying dormant, only to be shaken out of their sleep to be exposed and harass me.

Perhaps the comfortable life I spoke of earlier served as more of a mask that covered up what was really going on inside. Maybe, those comforts just allowed me to be comfortable in my discomfort. Perhaps the birthday invitation conversations served as a catalyst for me to deal with what was really going on, which takes me back to one of my original questions: what does success at 40 look like? Again, on paper and by most standards, I was successful. But in reality, I felt very far from it. I love what Andy Stanley says in his book, *Visioneering*. "It is no accident that you are where you are. And it is not necessarily a problem that you are not where you assume you ought to be."

I found Andy's statement liberating. I encourage you, I challenge you, no I dare you to free yourself from thinking that it's a problem that you are not where you assumed you would or should be in life. Take back the false idea and message that you have been rehearsing that says you have failed because you aren't where you thought you would be. Cancel the lie that whispers to you that it's too late or you just need to move on to something that is less than your true heart's desire.

There I was, feeling that there were too many empty boxes left to check off my mental checklist. Too many unconnected dots from where I was to where I assumed I would be. By age 40, I had assumed that I would be "successful." Although life was "good," there were many things that I assumed I would have accomplished, obtained and conquered. Yet still, these things remained a distant mirage.

I didn't quite know what was waiting for me when I reached that mirage in the distance. All I knew were the internal nudges, tugs and taps telling me, "there's more." All I knew was this feeling of success that I thought should be achieved by 40, wasn't anywhere in sight for me. Soon, I would discover that the main ingredient for real success was missing —and that was purpose.

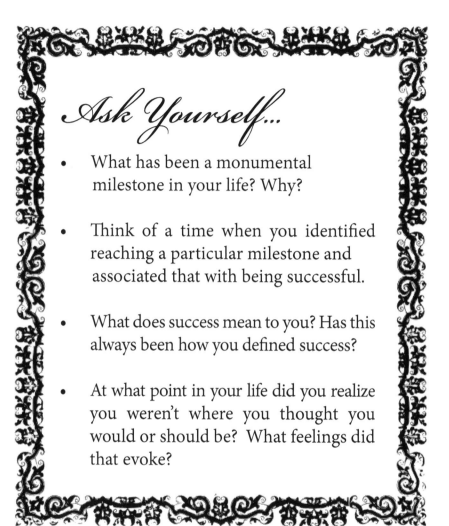

Ask Yourself...

- What has been a monumental milestone in your life? Why?

- Think of a time when you identified reaching a particular milestone and associated that with being successful.

- What does success mean to you? Has this always been how you defined success?

- At what point in your life did you realize you weren't where you thought you would or should be? What feelings did that evoke?

*"The meaning of life is to find your gift.
The purpose of life is to give it away."*

African Proverb

chapter3

*discovering
purpose*

Chapter 3:
Discovering Purpose

No matter the level of comfort that we experience, if our success isn't attached to purpose, we will continue to struggle and feel the internal nudges, tugs and whispers that "there is more." Deep down inside, there's an uneasiness that requires attention.

The fact remained that I couldn't answer the questions that were replaying in my head. The unchecked boxes in my life at the ripe age of forty included: "What about the books you were supposed to have written by now? What about all the nationwide speaking engagements? Where are all the people that were supposed to be booking you? What about the TV show? Where's the big office building? Where's the staff? Weren't you planning on getting your doctorate?

But I had to ask myself, "why?" Why did I feel I needed to accomplish all these things at 40?

Checking The Boxes

*F*or women, our empty "unchecked boxes" all look different, but yet are all the same. The boxes represent something that we want to accomplish or assumed we would have accomplish by a particular time frame, such as the desire to get married, to start a family, to work less and stay home more and for some, to work more and stay at home less. Some boxes are to lose a certain amount of weight, to purchase a dream home, to make a certain income, to finish school, to go back to school, to get certified, to launch a dream career, to purchase a home, to become an entrepreneur, to start a non-profit or to go into ministry. But in the wider scheme of things, these boxes don't matter. As a matter of fact, they're not real. As soon as you check one off another one pops up, and they continue to pop up and we find ourselves on a never-ending chase to check off the boxes and scratch off the item on the bucket list.

As women, we are often torturing ourselves by giving ourselves these mental milestones, timelines and deadlines. We give ourselves a case of the "should be." We often tell ourselves, "By the time I (fill in the blank), I should be (whatever it is you thought you would be doing or would have). I hear women talk about it all the time:

- "By the time I turn 26, I should be married."
- "By the time I turn 28, I should have my first child."
- "By the time I turn 33, I should be done with kids."
- "By the time I finish graduate school, I should be 25."

- "By the time I turn 35, I should have made partner."
- "By the time my kids finish school I should be ready to retire."
- "By the time I'm 30, I should be purchasing my first home."
- "I should be making six-figures by the time I'm 40."
- "I should be back to my pre-pregnancy size in three months."

I'm not sure what your "by the time I" has been, but our success is often dictated by how many boxes we've checked off. We determine how successful we are if we meet these mental deadlines.

What has success meant to you? When did you consider yourself successful? Will you be successful when you marry, have a child, move up on the corporate ladder, have a certain title or position, make partner at the law firm, have your own practice or business, go back into the workforce from staying at home, a promotion, recognition, have a couple extra 0's behind your savings, purchase your dream home, take fancy vacations, have all your major bills paid off, purchase the car you've been dying to have or lose the extra baby weight that you've been working on for the past several years?

Let me be very clear, there's nothing wrong with setting goals and looking forward to having nice things in life. I don't want to downplay or minimize pursuing your list of goals and aspirations. There's nothing wrong with having a plan and a vision and working hard and accomplishing those things that you desire. However, when these things become the sole benchmark for what success looks like, we can end up missing out. We're often confused and lack fulfillment because although life may look fine on paper, we won't be able to dodge and get away from the inner nudge and tug that there is "more" if we're not engaging our purpose.

Think about it, how many people do you know, personally or from afar, that had everything going on for them. They had all the trophies that come with having a successful life, as society defines it – money, recognition, status, the house, the car, the family, and everything else that spells out success. However, they find themselves in the most unfortunate of situations, by their own hands. By no means am I judging, but in many of those cases, although they gained the world, there's still a feeling of loss because they never found their purpose.

IN SEARCH OF PURPOSE

The only real box that we should be striving to check off is the box that says, "Connect with God-given purpose" and "Living my purpose." Once that box is checked, it brings meaning, satisfaction and joy to all the other boxes. These boxes serve as our voice and identity, which is the essence of our being. There aren't too many things in life more important than understanding and operating in your God-given purpose. We can have what appears to be success, but if it isn't attached to purpose, if it lacks significance or substance, we remain on the proverbial hamster wheel continuing to seek, but never reaching success. Too often we get to the end of our life and realize that it lacked a true purpose. Purpose gives us meaning. It serves as your "why," and it gives you a reason to not just live, but to want to live because of something far greater than yourself.

I now see and understand that my success was never dictated or predicated by those milestones. I am content with all the unchecked and empty boxes. I recognize now that even if I had accomplished all those things, without true purpose attached to it, I still wouldn't be successful. When I'm walking in the destiny of my God-given purpose, that purpose will always trump any milestones or check box that I could ever put on myself or allow society to dictate for me.

A CALL REVEALS PURPOSE

Several years back I began a prayer call that was geared for a specific group of women. Once those calls eventually ended, I felt the nudge for several years later to start another weekly prayer call, but this time, it would be open for anyone. I eventually followed through with the idea, got the word out about the calls and provided a platform for people to dial in on Monday mornings to hear a quick devotion and prayer as a way to jump start their day and their week.

A few months into the prayer calls, I started to feel frustrated and overwhelmed with trying to find someone each week to hold these short calls. I would always provide the lesson and prayer at least one week out of the month and then look for other leaders who would like to join in for the other remaining weeks of the month. This wasn't a huge task if I mapped out each month and lined up my speakers in advance. However, when you're like me and procrastinate and wait until you are a day or two out from the call and have to stress and go into panic mode to find someone to lead the call, it began to get a little overwhelming.

Several times I almost ended the prayer calls. I would make up in my mind, "okay, at the end of this month, I am going to make an announcement that we will no longer have the calls." But every time I would decide that I was going to end the calls, someone would text me or email me to say how much they appreciated the weekly calls and just how much of an impact the calls had on their life. Then they would conclude by saying something like, "Please don't ever stop with the calls. People really need them." Of course, I would then feel bad about considering to bring the calls to an end. It served as a reminder that it wasn't about me. Every time I got ready to "close shop," someone would pop out of nowhere to remind me how the calls impacted them. This made me realize that I couldn't stop. I was reminded that someone needed the very thing that I was providing. On one particular occasion, I was right back at my wits end with this prayer call thing! Organizing and scheduling people was becoming more of a task instead of joy. Once again, I said, "okay, I will finish out the month of June and then I am not going to resume with the calls."

The very next day, I received a call from someone who I didn't know. She told me her name and tried to jog my memory on who she was. She began the call with saying that she just wanted to thank me. At this point, I am totally confused as to what she is referring to. This was someone whom I met several years ago and probably had all of three conversations. I asked her what was she thanking me for. At that moment, she began to hysterically cry. She continued by saying how for months she has been receiving my weekly emails that I sent as a reminder of the Monday morning prayer calls. She told me that she had never called in to see what it was all about. But this particular day, she decided to call in and listen.

As she continued to cry, she said, "I just want you to know that my husband and I were planning on going to see our lawyers this week to file for a divorce. Your call touched me so much that I found the nerve to share with my husband what the call was about. So I'm calling to tell you "thank you," because instead of going to our lawyer's office this week, we've decided to go to our church marriage counselor's office instead." She continued to sob, and told me to "please don't stop what you are doing. You are helping to save people."

Now that call really convicted me. Here I was, once again, ready to close shop with these calls, not realizing that because of those calls, that I was "helping to save people." You see, this business of purpose is far greater than us. Those prayer calls were making a difference in the lives of people and making an impact far greater than I realized. I was playing a role in someone else's success and their lives were being changed. Again, our success is tied to our purpose. Although I mentally planned and attempted to stop the prayer calls, I was reminded of the good work that those calls were providing and that keeping those calls alive was a part of my own success story.

SIMPLE QUESTION FROM A MENTOR

As I was quickly approaching forty, I was flushing out all of my feelings and discontent with life with my dear friend and mentor, Denise. She helped me to peel back the layers on all that I was feeling. My friend, in all her wisdom, asked me one question: Do you feel that you have made a difference in your home and community? This didn't necessarily seem to be the question I would expect from her. However, I paused and thought it out. Although I wasn't where I assumed I would be in life, with all of my unchecked boxes, I believed that I had made somewhat of a difference in my home and community. After I thought about that, I then answered her with "YES!"

My mentor smiled and said, "when we honor God with our lives and use what He has given us to make a difference, then you are successful." In that instant, I felt free. My outlook and definition of success had been redefined in a five-minute conversation. As simple as that seemed, and as complex as I was making it before, not only did it shed light on my perception of success, but it set me free from all the weight and guilt I had put on myself. I was successful for no other reason than because I had the ability to use my God given gifts to make an impact and a difference in the lives of others. I celebrate the fact that I don't have to live in torment and disappointment anymore, because I don't have to live up to the self-inflicted expectation of all that "should be" and the unchecked boxes of life.

I encourage and challenge you to also resolve the issue that you have to do something groundbreaking, make headline news, or discover the cure for diseases or world peace to find success. I have resolved the false notion of having to "do" and I am content on just being right where I am in life. When I am living in my God given design and purpose, I don't have to go looking for validation. Instead, I get to create my own success. Success is already within. Success is not "outside of you," it's "inside you."

It Is Not About You

our purpose is not about you. It is in essence about others and how you will serve others with all of your unique gifts, abilities, skills and experiences in a way that is bigger than you. Purpose answers the single question of "How is someone else's life better because of me?" But even more so, how does my impact influence others to be better in life? We were all born with a specific God-given purpose and plan. In fact, before you were born, you were already chosen with a purpose. Fulfilling that purpose and plan must be our primary mission in life.

When we learn to walk into our purpose, it gives our lives meaning, significance, fulfillment, peace and joy. Living a life where we are detached and disconnected from our purpose creates torment, anguish, frustration, emptiness, anxiety, a never ending hunger, a void and the constant nudge and tug that something is missing. We attempt to fill that vacancy and void with things, people, habits and new ideas that at best, only serves as a temporary fix.

We were each given a divine assignment, a reason for being, a way to be a solution and our "why" that gives us meaning, significance and value. But even more importantly, that gives meaning, significance and value to others and the world around us. I'm grateful to have connected with and be in constant pursuit of my own purpose. This book is a reflection of that purpose, which we will discuss more in chapters to come.

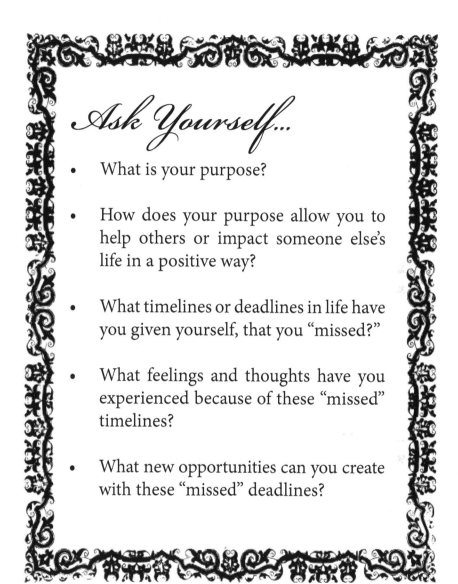

Ask Yourself...

- What is your purpose?

- How does your purpose allow you to help others or impact someone else's life in a positive way?

- What timelines or deadlines in life have you given yourself, that you "missed?"

- What feelings and thoughts have you experienced because of these "missed" timelines?

- What new opportunities can you create with these "missed" deadlines?

"When I stand before God at the end of my life, I would hope that I would not have a single bit of talent and could say, I used everything you gave me."

Erma Bombeck

chapter4

create your legacy

CHAPTER 4:
Create Your Legacy

s I searched for my purpose, it became clear that there was another reason for the tugging and nudging inside me. I wanted to be known for something. I wanted to make an impact on the world. I wanted to help others. But just as important, truth be told, I wanted to be successful in my own right, on my own terms and known for something far greater than being "Tracy McGrady's wife" or "TMac's wife," the wife of a superstar. As awesome of an athlete and person my husband is, I still needed to know that I had my own legacy to leave. I didn't want to just be impressive, I wanted to be impactful. That's why writing this book, and books to come, is so important to me. This is a part of my legacy.

Whether you are the wife of an athlete, a plumber, an

attorney, an engineer or a teacher, or not a wife at all, as women our dreams often are overshadowed by the husband, children, aging parents, the job or the day-to-day rigors of life. If we don't recognize it soon enough, we find ourselves putting our dreams on the back burner or never pursuing them at all. With the celebrity factor surrounding my husband in the earlier part of his career, I found that I quickly lost my identity and my voice. It began with a situation that others created, but soon became something that I played into and perpetuated. What I mean is, when you are married to a public figure, unless you are already established with your own platform, or you are a public figure yourself, people don't recognize you for who you are. They don't understand that you are your own person. They don't even acknowledge you by your name – you actually become nameless. For quite some time, I was "Tracy McGrady's wife." I would have people introduce me and make introductions as: "This is Tracy McGrady's wife." I couldn't even get my name tagged on the end: "This is Tracy McGrady's wife, CleRenda." I was strictly the wife of a star. I, unfortunately, decided to give up my career and the things that were important for me, which meant giving up my identity and my voice.

Although the problem began with people only seeing me as "Tracy McGrady's wife," I perpetuated the problem by playing right into it and literally becoming "just his wife." Don't get me wrong. My husband is amazing and the joy and love of my life. It is my joy and honor to be his wife. However, I had disconnected with who I was. I wasn't actively engaging in my purpose or creating my own story apart from him. My legacy, at that point, didn't extend beyond being "just his wife." I had the stuff, status, stature, and been around the stardom. Yet, with all of the bells and whistles that most associate with success, I continued to feel a void because there was no significance or purpose tied to it.

Stuff doesn't necessarily mean success. We live in a culture that says the bigger, better and more stuff that you accumulate, means you have arrived. There is nothing wrong with having nice things. I love nice things. The problem comes in when we think the stuff in life will bring us fulfillment and somehow give us meaning and purpose. Chasing after material things alone will never fill the voids that we often experience when our soul is yearning for something greater.

So for a season of my life, before I was re-connected with my own identity and purpose, my success was predicated upon my husband's success. My identity was wrapped in his identity. It wasn't intentional and I certainly hadn't planned or wanted it that way, but I had adopted the mindset and beliefs of others around me. Being the wife of a seven-time NBA All-star who was once one of the top three players in the league, I was the epitome of what some would say: "success looks like that."

However, under the mask that we women can wear, behind my Hermes purse, Red Bottom shoes and 30,000-square-foot home, was a woman who struggled with two major things that kept me from connecting with my true purpose. Those two things were losing my own identity and voice because of my lifestyle, and then secretly dealing with fear of failure, doubt and insecurity that had plagued me much of my life - to do the things that I really knew I was called to do and wanted to do.

I thought for quite some time that my success would come by way of my husband. That somehow success would just magically appear for me, as a result of my marriage. I ultimately knew that I was destined for my own greatness, on my own merit, but it was buried so deep inside me that I forgot who I was. I chose to live in my comfort zone, which eventually became uncomfortable. It's these uncomfortable moments of life that become our wake-up call.

In my spirit, I knew that I was CleRenda McGrady, author, speaker, TV host, and world changer. However, my mind was just slow to believe it and my heart had yet to receive it. I don't mean to sound negative, ungrateful or that I had it bad somehow. However, anytime you walk away from who you are - your dreams, desires, goals and purpose in life - you take the risk of walking in the shadow of someone else. Once this takes place, your personal identity becomes lost. Once you lose your identity, you lose your voice. Once you've lost your identity and voice, you lose your impact and you compromise your own power and what you have to bring to the table. And that's exactly what became my story. I lost my identity, I lost my voice and I lost my power. If we lose our identity, our voice and our impact, how can we live and leave a legacy? However, like all things lost, they can be found again. In order to have a legacy, you must maintain your own personal identity, or at least, go back and find it.

TO KNOW THY SELF

I was talking to a businesswoman once who had a high-powered corporate career – a very coveted position. But as a corporate executive for a Fortune 500 company and well known in her industry – she was miserable. It wasn't her purpose. She told me she felt as if she was just going through the motions. What she really wanted was to use her talent and gifts to create a center for children with disabilities. Unfortunately, her family and friends didn't share her vision and couldn't understand how important this dream was to her. They told her she was crazy for even thinking about abandoning such a lucrative career and all of her achievements. To them, "to venture off and do this side thing full time" didn't make sense. For her, there was no fulfillment in being a corporate executive because in her heart, she was somewhere totally different. She wasn't using her gifts in a way she felt created change.

Even her parents questioned her judgement – what about all the degrees, everything they had sacrificed to send her to an elite school. How could she just quit and leave it all behind? They also reminded her how walking away from such an esteemed position would affect her legacy. And so, she ultimately left her executive position. But again, our success is not bound by the definition and expectations of others. Her only regret: that she stayed longer than she wanted because of the guilt and pressure that she felt from the outside. Our success is about how we use our gifts to make an impact and create change. Ultimately, our efforts become our legacy. The impact and change that we make and leave behind is how we are remembered. In order to leave a legacy, we must be living one.

The courage and boldness that the lady exemplified in making a decision to push through, prevented her from conforming to the success narrative of others. By doing this, she decided on what her legacy would be. Her legacy will now go down in history as selflessly transforming the lives of children with disabilities, so that they recognize and are inspired and empowered by their abilities. Now that's what I call making an impact.

It is your birthright to walk into the fullness of the destiny that you have been created for, called for and chosen for. Before you were ever in your mama's belly, before you were a dot on the ultrasound machine, you were chosen with purpose to do mighty work. Your legacy is to provide something that goes far beyond your title, career or position, and one that will go far beyond your time on Earth.

We don't always get that. We think: "that's for others, but not for me." There are things that attempt to derail us, and keep us from operating in our birthright. However, we must be diligent in pushing past those things and be steadfast in our purpose in order to create our legacy. We seem to think "others" are the ones qualified and equipped to live a life of purpose and to leave behind a legacy. We don't always see ourselves as equal or having the same ability to do something great and meaningful with our lives. Everyone has a sphere of influence. Although one person may have a greater and wider reach, everyone has the ability and opportunity on some level to touch someone else. You can begin the journey of creating your legacy as early as childhood or teenage years, or later in adulthood. But life can get in the way, take you down different paths, create detours that can take you so far from your dream that it becomes a distant memory.

Olympic gold medalist Simone Biles embraced her dream early in life. She was flipping around the house as a young girl and when exposed to gymnastics during an unscheduled field trip, she knew it was her calling. As a teenager, she found herself at a crossroad where she had to decide whether or not to pursue her dream of becoming an Olympic athlete, which meant choosing to be home-schooled, or to go to the local high school with her friends. She hated being home-schooled, but her hard work paid off when she won four gold medals and one bronze at the 2016 Olympics in Brazil.

Also at the 2016 Summer Olympics in Rio de Janeiro was 30-year-old Gwen Jorgensen, who went on to win the gold medal in the triathlon event for the United States. Jorgensen attended the University of Wisconsin-Madison where she ran and swam for the Badgers and then went on to earn a master's degree in accounting and pass the CPA exam. She was a tax accountant for Ernst & Young in Milwaukee when she got the call from USA Triathlon. She took a chance at pursuing her dream of becoming an Olympic athlete and after long hours of training, sacrifice, and the will to push through, she created her own legacy.

Their stories alone have allowed young girls and women to not only dream, but to dream again. To pick that dream off the shelf, blow the dust off and go get it. Their drive and determination to push beyond all obstacles and setbacks has placed them in a pool of many whose legacies will forever impact others.

In his book, *The Difference You Make,* leadership expert Pat Williams says: "…we all have influence, we all have an impact on the people around us and we have all been shaped and impacted by the influencers in our own lives." Too often we think in terms of "little ole me" and assume those with larger-than-life platforms and even larger audiences are the only ones who can leave a legacy. However, from Biblical times on up to present day, many times it's the "little ones," who weren't qualified or equipped who actually alter the trajectory of history – bringing change to their communities and societies.

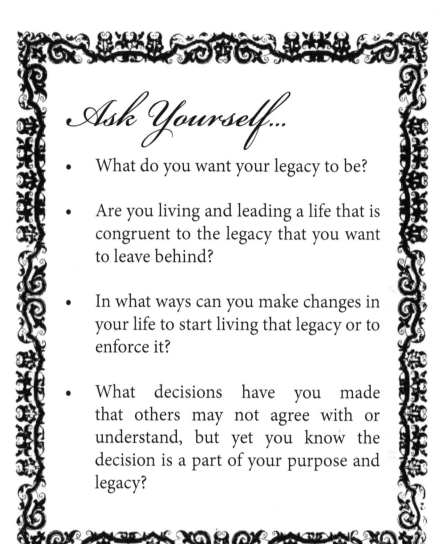

Ask Yourself...

- What do you want your legacy to be?

- Are you living and leading a life that is congruent to the legacy that you want to leave behind?

- In what ways can you make changes in your life to start living that legacy or to enforce it?

- What decisions have you made that others may not agree with or understand, but yet you know the decision is a part of your purpose and legacy?

"Every strike brings me closer to the next home run."

Babe Ruth

chapter5

what's in your hands?

CHAPTER 5:
What's in Your Hands?

I love reading the account of Moses and all of his conversations of doubt concerning his ability and qualifications for being the one chosen to free the Israelites out of slavery in Egypt.

I actually kind of chuckle because I imagine myself with his exact concerns and questions: "How am I supposed to do that?" "Who am I to guide them?" "What happens if it doesn't work out?" In the midst of Moses' fear and frustration regarding what he didn't have and why he couldn't go forth with the task at hand, God asked Moses one question that changed everything: "What is that in your hand?" The Lord showed Moses that the rod he carried in his hand was anointed with power to enable Moses to go forth and fulfill his calling and to do the things that he wouldn't ordinarily be able to do with his own strength.

Immediately Moses took his mind from what he couldn't do and what he didn't have and focused his attention to what he had in his hand and what he was now able to do. Moses realized that God had already prepared and positioned him to accomplish what he was called to do. The rod was the tool God equipped Moses with to do every unimaginable task that Moses faced. Many of us are just like Moses. We focus on our perceived inabilities and what we can't do or what we don't have access to. We focus on how "it" didn't work for us in the past. However, we can't despair over lost opportunities or failed attempts. We will never create our success story by lamenting over past failures and regrets of what could have and should have been.

Let's use the same simple question to shift us from where we are to where we want to be. You have a lot more "in your hands" than you realize. What you already have is all you need to begin to change your life and the lives of others around you. In evaluating what you have, your mind only wants to see the "good stuff." But it's those struggles, regrets and painful seasons in our lives that can be used as the catalyst that propels us to our next level of greatness.

As we consider what we have in our hands, I challenge you not to discount the pain, hurt and disappointments of life. Those experiences are in your hands for a reason. Our purpose often comes from our pain. Our breakthroughs may come from those breakups, breakdowns and breaking points in life. Nothing goes wasted. There is purpose behind everything that we experience. It doesn't mean we will always understand why we're going through challenges and storms, but those times are part of our story and help to create, shape and mold who we are and the path that we take. If we choose to connect with our purpose, use what's in our hands and discover how all the "bad" can be used for "good," then we can create our own success story and encourage others to do the same.

Use What You Have

*S*uccess comes down to how we operate and walk in our purpose. Purpose is simply how we use our God given talents, skills and strengths to make a difference in the world. It's how we allow God to use us to serve and be a solution in the world. We're successful when we're operating in our God-given purpose, as we use what we have, right where we're at, as we continue to evolve into who God is calling us to be. According to leadership guru, Fred Smith, "the measurement of success is simply the ratio of talents used to talents received."

Speaking of talents, what better story to illustrate this concept than the parable of the rich ruler and his servant. The "Parable of the Talents" in Matthew 25:14–30 tells of a master who, before leaving his house for travel, entrusted his property to his three servants. Each servant was given one or more talents – a significant amount of money – in accordance to their abilities. After a long absence, the master returned home and rewarded the two servants that used their talents and punished the third servant who didn't use his talent at all.

The servants, who did the most they could with what the master had given them, were the ones who were successful. Although the servants did not have equal talents, the two faithful servants doubled the portion they started out with. They invested and utilized well, what they had. However, the servant who did nothing with his talent, who basically sat on it, played it safe and chose not to be faithful with what God had asked him to do, was unsuccessful in God's eyes. He chose to do nothing with what he had. We each have our own talents, abilities, skills and experiences. It's how we use those gifts that determine the impact we have on the world and others around us.

YOU ARE UNIQUE

The world needs something that only you can provide in the unique manner in which you were created, designed and destined to give. Although there are plenty of other people that may have similar abilities, no one can do "it" in the way you were chosen to do so.

Your purpose allows you to use all your unique gifts, talents, abilities and experiences (good and bad) in a way that is beyond who you are, and how you may influence the world around you. Your purpose is about how you are uniquely equipped to impact others. You were called to play a role on Earth. Your life will completely change when you learn and live your purpose. Many of you may think, "well I already know my purpose." However, the work of purpose is progressive - it's ongoing and continues to go deeper as the years go on. If you are clear on your purpose, the task at hand is to continue to grow with it and find the "what's next."

We must stay diligent. We do ourselves and everyone else around us a disservice when we don't live in our purpose. Live out your purpose, don't take it to the grave. The late great Dr. Myles Munroe said, "the greatest tragedy in life is not death, but a life without purpose." So in order for me to avoid that "greatest tragedy," I had to acknowledge that internal void and hone in on my God-given purpose. How was I using my gifts, talents and abilities to make a difference in the lives of others?

As I pondered this question, I realized that God had been preparing and molding me – actually pushing me – outside of my comfort zone, to use my voice. Whether it was through writing or speaking, my purpose is to encourage and inspire people, in particular, women, to live a life of fulfillment and significance by living in their purpose. My purpose was to help others connect with their purpose and to live a life that represented their biggest vision and best version of themselves.

I'm around a lot of women, and in sharing and talking to women from all walks-of-life, I started to realize that we all have similar internal struggles. These struggles typically deal with the "check the box syndrome." For whatever reason, whether it's fear, insecurity, doubt and feelings of inadequacy, even when we are able to check off all of the boxes, we can still experience a void. We attempt to fill it with material things, people, projects, habits, but the void remains, until we fill it with what it's supposed to be filled with – our purpose. It was time for me to fill my own voids, embrace my purpose and create my own success, according to how I defined it.

PERFECT TIMING

*N*o matter how hard we try, many of us have been known to back down from our God-given dreams, give up on hope and give up on our dream. But you are right where you need to be. God is using you right where you are. What you are going through is positioning you to walk in the purpose He has for your life. Your current situation is part of the plan He has for you. You have not lost time, you are not wasting your time, and time has not gotten away from you. In fact, if you're living a life of your God-given purpose, or willing to pick up from where you are now, then you are actually in "perfect" time. The clock may be ticking, but you have not timed out! God's timing is not our timing and you have been positioned where you are for such a time as this.

In the midst of what appears not to be working for us, the God of the universe is working strategically behind the scenes, working everything out for our good. God is laying the ground work in us – pruning, shaping, correcting, molding and maturing us – so that we can be the best version of ourselves, in order to properly fulfill the role that is set before us. I know that there have been things that I wanted and even thought I deserved. However, looking back, had those doors opened, I would have blown it because I wasn't ready. Just because we feel we "deserve" something, doesn't equate to actually being ready to receive it. There have been occasions in my life when I couldn't understand why I didn't get what I thought I should. I now understand that I needed to be groomed more, stretched more and shaped more in certain areas.

I challenge you to embrace and celebrate who you are, right now — shortcomings, failed attempts, lost opportunities and all. These areas of life are all a part of our story. God not only uses your gifts, talents and passion, but He also uses your mistakes, challenges and mess-ups as a part of your cause and purpose. Once we change our perception, we will recognize that these areas and moments in our lives are not setbacks, but they are actually "set-ups." These seasons of frustration where it appears that things are going every which way but the "right way," are actually positioning us and setting us up for something greater.
It's easy to be tempted to look at everyone else and believe everything just magically works for them. Although we may not be where we want to be or have access to everything we

would like, when we shift our focus to what we do have, we invite in possibilities and recognize that everything we need is closer than we think. You can create what you need and desire right from what's inside your hand. So ask yourself: "What's in your hand?"

Ask Yourself...

- What are your talents, gifts, abilities and things that you do very well?

- What abilities do you have that others compliment you on?

- How have you aligned your talents with you purpose?

- What hardships or challenges have you experienced, but later it was used for something good or for an opportunity?

"The two most important days in your life is the day you were born and the day you find out why."

Mark Twain

chapter6

making the connection

CHAPTER 6:
Making the Connection

A turning point for me – when getting serious about this matter of connecting with my purpose –was an event that I experienced on a family summer trip.

The destination for our family summer vacation was the same Caribbean island that we had come to know and love for the past several years. In addition to all the wonderful amenities, friendly staff and beautiful and relaxing beaches, one of the anticipated highlights of the trip was "the parade," which took place once a week on the resort grounds. The parade took on a Brazilian Carnival theme – captivating music, over the top costumes and contagious energy that everyone looked forward to.

There was a wave of people migrating to the front of the

resort, scrambling to get the coveted "front row" spots. We weren't any different; managing to get the perfect location. Soon, from a distance, we heard the vibrating beats of the steel drums, the piercing squeals of the horns and the high-pitched screeches of the men and women in the parade. Tapping my foot to the beat, I knew that in a moment the parade would be upon us.

As the parade drew near, I picked up the intensity of my movements, until I was dancing along on the curbside, waving and cheering the parade participants on as they danced past us. The costumes were exotic, the headpieces were mesmerizing and their body movements were in rhythm with the beat of the instruments. After a few minutes, I was so consumed by the parade that I didn't notice the other spectators slowly – one by one – starting to leave the area. The music that was loud, vibrant and ringing in my ears was now fading in the distance. At this point, all I saw was the back of the parade. I assumed that another round of the parade would soon arrive, so I began to wait with great anticipation. Most of the people had cleared the area and my family was growing irritated with me as I continued to wait for the next procession.

Surely, this couldn't be the end of the parade. Was no one else as concerned as I was? Didn't anyone see this as a problem? I became frustrated and immediately asked my husband, "what's going on? It's not over, is it?" He didn't give me the answer that I wanted, so I asked one of the other bystanders leaving the area. "Excuse me, is this it? Is the parade over?" Again, the answer she gave me wasn't what I wanted to hear.

I went on a mini rampage, searching for someone, anyone who could reassure me that the parade wasn't over and "yes," there's more to come. I finally waved down one of the resort staff to ask him about the parade. Frantically I asked him, "Is that it, is the parade over? There's more, right?"

I can't recall what the resort assistant said, but what I will always remember is what I heard – a voice speaking to me. No, this wasn't an audible voice; it was something that I "heard" within. Something that spoke to my inner being and to the depths of my soul in a way that no audible voice would ever be able to speak to me. This voice commanded my attention. No longer was I vexed and intoxicated about the rest of the parade. Now my attention shifted elsewhere and the questions were directed back to me...
Is it over?
Is that it?
Is there more to you?

I felt like I was in a trance or that I was experiencing some weird, out of body moment. Not fully understanding what had come over me, or what this paralyzing feeling was all about, the voice grew louder and more direct. "CleRenda! Is it over for YOU? Is that it for YOU? Is there more to YOU?"

I started to think about my own life, and it was from that moment I started to ask myself the same questions every day. Once we returned home from vacation, I couldn't forget the experience. All of the questions that I was asking pertaining to the parade were questions that were meant for me personally. Just like I was a spectator on the sidelines watching the parade go by, I had become a spectator in my own life.

I was comfortable watching my life from the sidelines and not working towards my dreams and God-given purpose in life. I wasn't living my best version and vision of myself. I was letting fear, insecurity and doubt rob me of going forth and pursuing my calling in life. As a matter of fact, not only was I robbing myself, but I later discovered I was robbing others of what I had to contribute to the world.

Of all the many gifts and abilities that I knew God entrusted me with to go forth and make a difference, somewhere along the way I chose to sit on them and bury them.

Project P.U.S.H.!

Most of my light bulb moments, ideas and revelations happen while in the shower. So much so, that I keep a notepad on a table right outside my shower door so I can reach out, dripping wet, and capture a thought. If not, the moment will come quick and leave even faster. As a matter of fact, my purpose was "given" to me in the shower.

The majority of this book was created right there in the shower, before I ever made it to the computer. Most of my thoughts and content was a result of me standing half way out of the shower, writing on my notepad. The pages would get worn and wrinkly from the dripping water, but it was my way of capturing my thoughts before they slipped away.

On one odd occasion, my spirit was spoken to in my backyard while watching my kids play. Out of nowhere, a vision flashed across my mind. The word "push" had always been a special word for me. Without much thought or effort, the word went from just a word to an acronym full of life and meaning. One by one, I thought of new words that gave the word "push" a whole new meaning.

I have always loved acronyms, so it was very fitting that what would become the start of a movement for me, came in the form of an acronym: P-Purpose-led. U-Unstoppable. S-Success-bound. H-Hope-filled. I didn't know what all of that meant, but it sounded amazing and it felt right. All I knew was in that moment, there was a shift. I conceived my purpose, which would allow me to give birth to that vision and create my own success story.

As with many of our purposes, mine started off as my personal dilemma and struggle. Our purpose often emerges out of pain, problems, and hardships. For me, I was sick of always feeling pregnant with this purpose, but too fearful, too insecure and too doubtful to push it out.

So out of the pain, void, tugs, aches, and the inability to activate and actualize my dreams, I found the catalyst for my own purpose — to inspire other women to move beyond the self-limiting and sabotaging beliefs that we carry around, connect with their purpose and fulfill their dreams.

Many of you are like I was: Pregnant with purpose, dreams, visions and ideas but can't go forth and "push thru" and give birth because of fear and other things that block us. When we don't give birth to that purpose, we abandon the dream, lose the excitement and conform to a smaller version of who we really are. So this is why Project P.U.S.H.! was created. It was an answer to my own problem. I figured if I struggled with giving birth to my dreams, then possibly others may have that same struggle.

This is why and how I embraced my own purpose. It became my deepest desire to help other women push through the obstacles that may hold them back from pursuing their purpose. As I continue to become Purpose-led, Unstoppable, Success-bound and Hope-filled, I want other women to do the same, so that together, we are fulfilling our dreams and creating our own success story. We must release ourselves from the burden and weight of being captive to the pressures of society – that we have to prove our worth and our significance in order to showcase our success.

Until we connect with our God-given purpose, the internal tugging and warring within you won't stop until you acknowledge it and do something about it. In the meantime, what we can do is "P.U.S.H." Let's break down the acronym further. Allow this to serve as a "creed" to remind us as often as needed, that we all have a greater purpose and calling to fulfill, regardless of what's going on around us or inside of us.

P.U.S.H. – Purpose-led, Unstoppable, Success-bound and Hope-filled

Purpose-led	*"I have been set apart, predestined, chosen, created and appointed with a purpose that only I can go forth and deliver. I am Purpose-led!"*
Unstoppable	*"I am strong, courageous, confident and bold! My spirit is not timid, fearful or afraid. I have been chosen as a vessel to do great works and I will not be stopped! I am UnStoppable!"*
Success-bound	*"I have been divinely chosen for plans of hope and a good future that will prosper me in ways that far exceed more than I could ask or imagine. My success allows me to make a difference and impact the lives and success of others! I am Success-bound!"*
Hope-filled	*"I will not allow my current circumstances and the things that I can see to cause me to waiver on the hope and promises that are already carved out for me. My hope anchors me and I choose to believe and anticipate that which is already mine. I am Hope-filled!"*

PURPOSE-LED

You were chosen and created with a purpose in mind. You were created to do something and to give something to the world that only you can provide in the authentic way that is unique to you. Your purpose allows you to use all the unique gifts, talents, abilities, and good and bad experiences in a way that is beyond who you are, but to be used in a way that will impact and influence others.

UNSTOPPABLE

There are so many things tugging at our attention that attempt to stop us from walking in our authentic power and achieving our dreams and desires. If we aren't intentional, we will fall prey to the limiting and sabotaging beliefs that whisper to us that we can't, we shouldn't or that it's impossible to achieve. It's time to live beyond the limits and boundaries that have stopped you and kept you from pursuing your dreams and living a more meaningful life.

SUCCESS-BOUND

Success in today's culture considers the outside more than the inside. As I said in Chapter 3, we allow the stuff, status, stature and stardom of life to dictate and define what success is and what it isn't. Although those things may be indicative of "surface success" and things acquired and accomplished, it doesn't necessarily mean "true success." True success is tied to your purpose. True success is more about significance and substance. It is when you use what you have to create change for others.

HOPE-FILLED

There are countless reasons that deceive us into thinking that we should throw in the towel, quit, do something different, scale back and abandon the dream. Great visions don't manifest themselves overnight. When our dreams are anchored in the hope and faith that whatever we put our mind to we can achieve it, we begin to invite possibilities back into our hearts. Our hope allows us to see the vision, and press forward.

P.U.S.H. has become the foundation for my philosophy – my mantra – toward life and living life to its fullest. When we are able to stand firm in what these words represent, then we are able to embrace the essence of who we are and why we are here.

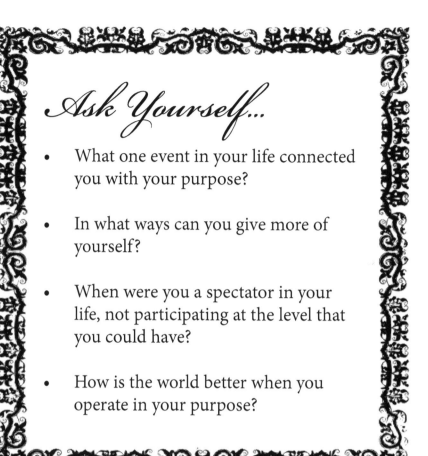

Ask Yourself...

- What one event in your life connected you with your purpose?

- In what ways can you give more of yourself?

- When were you a spectator in your life, not participating at the level that you could have?

- How is the world better when you operate in your purpose?

"Don't worry about the failures, worry about the chances you miss when you don't even try."

Jack Canfield

chapter7

redefining
success

CHAPTER 7:
Redefining Success

*N*ow that we have laid a strong foundation for what purpose is and how it's tied to our success, it's important that we consider closely – what is success?

To quote football legend, Tim Tebow: "Success comes in a lot of ways, but it doesn't come with money and it doesn't come with fame. It comes from having meaning in your life, doing what you love and being passionate about what you do. That's having a life of success. When you have the ability to do what you love, love what you do and have the ability to impact people. That's having a life of success. That's what having a life of meaning is."

In a nutshell, success is not about what you have, but how you passionately use what you have in an effort to make a difference and create change in the lives of others.

In a culture that worships the glitz, glam, glitter and overnight fame and fortune, our standard for success is often false, unobtainable and unrealistic. By no means am I suggesting there is anything wrong with having this kind of status. I think it is an incredibly amazing and admired opportunity, particularly when you use it to make a difference. My point, however, is that if our overall intention and motives are to strive to just be seen, adored, acknowledged and accumulate, but yet we bear no real fruit with real significance attached to it, then the true essence of success has not been achieved.

Take out the world's view of success and the pressure to conform. Take out the lies and misconceptions that say: you have to have the perfect look, the perfect record, the perfect house, the perfect spouse, the perfect kids, the perfect career or job, the perfect title, the perfect answer to the question, "what do you do," the perfect education, the perfect past, the perfect present, the perfect future, the perfect number of zeros in your bank account, the perfect achievements, the perfect status, and the perfect number of checked boxes to all the bucket list items that we assume we would accomplish within the perfect time frame.

Whhhheeew! I'm exhausted just thinking about it. You know you can have all that "perfection," and still allow success to slip through your fingers. Success looks, feels and sounds like something different to all of us, and we're motivated by our different views of it. It's important to define what success looks like for you — and you alone. When you don't conform to the world's definition of success and define it for yourself, you then begin to create your own success story.

You are going to achieve success much quicker once you've wrapped your head around what true success looks like. Better yet, you may just realize that you have already achieved success and just didn't know it or haven't owned it. Don't let the world or your friends, today's trends and popular culture, family expectations, social media, reality TV, or the pressure to conform, dictate your success.

WHAT SUCCESS LOOKS LIKE

*A*s women, it's easy to fall victim to what success "should" look like, especially when we allow someone else to define it. We feel like we're failures or don't measure up, or that we are not close to where we should be in life if we haven't accomplished everything that the world says we should. We become a prime target for burn out, frustration and throwing in the towel, if we can't see, touch, and post pictures of "it" on social media. Until we can broaden our view of success, according to how we define it, we will stay limited, stuck and frustrated because we're attached to the outcome and not the experience.

When I started Project P.U.S.H. a few years ago, I wanted to help women who are called to a bigger vision and version of themselves to push beyond the areas that keep them stuck, so they can rise to their full potential and purpose. Ticket sales did not go the way I had hoped for my first event. I had to stop mid-stream, look inward and define what success looked like for me. My first thought was that I wanted a sell-out crowd with people standing around the perimeter because all the seats had been taken. I was so paranoid about it. But was that what I really wanted? Was that what success looked like for me, or was it more about what I perceived success looked like for others?

I had to realign my priorities and find, for me, what was most important. Was it for the seats to be filled; to recoup the cost and make a huge profit? Or was I going to be okay with the seats halfway filled, but knowing that I made an impact in someone's life – that someone would leave a little better than when they came. I wanted to know that I had inspired someone to push on into the next step of their dream that they had once abandoned.

So, as much as I wanted it to be a sell-out event (and it was), success for me was knowing that day made a difference; that the event was the catalyst to shift the audience into a different way of thinking, so that they would be inspired to push through to their next level. What was exciting was that I created my own terms on what success would look like for me and it was aligned with my true purpose.

Give yourself permission to reconsider and redefine success for you. We have to stop looking to others to approve, validate, and co-sign what we want our life to look like and represent. True success is more about significance and substance. It is about who you are and how you are using the talents you were given to make a difference in the world. Your success is personal and subjective to you. It's between you and God; how he wired you and commissioned you. Someone else's blueprint of success will look entirely different from yours. And that's okay.

IT'S NOT ABOUT THE PERKS

We get caught up in wrongly defining success with the tangible perks of success. We often misinterpret and measure success by these big ticket perk items that we discussed earlier — dream home, dream car, dream income and the list goes on. However, we can't afford to confuse true success with the tangible and visible perks of success. If we continue to rely on some kind of perk to validate and assure us of our success, then we will lose hope quickly, continue to feel an internal void and not truly capture the essence of what success is and what we have to offer. I do not mention the following to impress you, but merely to impress upon you the importance of living a life with purpose. I've lived in private communities and traveled by private planes and private chauffeurs, vacationed on private yachts and had private dinners by private chefs on private islands, and went on private shopping trips where I couldn't decide if I wanted the black, blue, beige or brown one – so I got all four!

But one thing I learned is that without knowing and living a life that reflected my greater divine purpose, as it relates to the identity of who I am and whose I am as a child of God and believer of Christ, all those private privileges only left me privately depressed, broken, insecure and seeking for something far greater to fill a void that no luxury would ever be able to fill. So when the world's view of that lifestyle assumes I should and would be at my fullest, I was at my emptiest.

Nothing is wrong with perks and nice things. The larger issue is when we allow the perks and stuff to define us. We can't find true fulfillment in these things. At best, they provide a temporary high, but once the novelty wears off, we find ourselves experiencing the same void. You don't have to have the trophies to prove that you are a winner. You don't need the ribbon to show that you crossed the finished line. No, the fact that you have committed yourself by connecting with and operating in your God-given purpose says it loud and clear – you are a winner.

I know so many people who I admire and deem successful, but yet they may not have the perks of life. In the same token, I know many people who have the perks, but yet they aren't successful.

One person that's high on my list of most "successful" people – although she didn't have the perks to show it – was my mother. I didn't realize it then but she planted a seed in me a long time ago, to help me understand what success really looks like. If there is such a thing as a hero, my mom was that in my life. So much of who I am today is shaped by her. She has gone on to glory, but in many ways she continues to shape me.

SUCCESS FOLLOWS PURPOSE

*L*ike we discussed earlier, success is tied to your purpose and it's all about finding joy in living a life of significance and meaning. For me, I'm successful when I consider who I am becoming, who I can impact, who I can inspire, who I can help bring transformation to, who I can serve, and how I use my time, talent and resources for a greater cause.

My mother spent 42 years of her life in ministry. She worked at a seminary where 80 percent of the students were from different countries around the world. These students attended the college so that they could return back to their country with a greater understanding, knowledge and awareness of the Bible and God. They utilized what they learned to build churches, teach the Gospel or go into ministry.

My mother had many roles at Winston-Salem Bible College. She served as the executive administrator to the president of the school; taught English, typing and Bible classes; led weekly chapel and served as student advisor. She also spent time with the students outside of the school, and took missions trips to their home countries.

Although my mother gave so much of herself to the college, I was always a little baffled by why she just didn't "get a real job." Friday was always "payday" – the day when most of my peers' parents were paid. I would sit on the side lines as my friends talked in great expectation of getting a new pair of shoes or gadget on Friday when their parent's received their pay check. I always envied the conversations. Friday at our house was just Friday. Many Fridays would come and go with my mom never seeing a paycheck. The Bible College that my mother worked for was a private faith-based institution and they relied on outside financial donations to not only meet the needs for the upkeep of the college, but for the salaries as well. Basically, my mother's "payday" depended on whether there were ample donations. If not, another week would go by without anything to show for it.

All this work and no pay. As a typical teenager, I became a little resentful of this work that she was so devoted to, as well as some of the students who she took in like her own.

My mother was a highly educated woman who was recruited several times by one of the larger and more coveted companies in our city. I just couldn't understand why she would choose to "settle," instead of pursuing a successful career with an established company that guaranteed "real pay" on a "real pay date."

As I began to grow and mature and connect more with my own bigger purpose in life, I often reflect back to something my mother wrote to me in a graduation card. "If you see a turtle on a post, you know he didn't get there on his own. Always give back to life the best way that you can."

At the time, those words were just words on a card. However, those words would later become more than just words to me.

They would become a foundational piece of who I am. Those words have shaped my views on what true success really is. True success is about service. It is about empowering others and using what you have to create change and ignite possibility into the lives of those around you. Today, I try to live by those words – always give back to life the best way that you can —not your neighbor, not the person on TV or social media, not who you thought you would have been twenty years ago, not who someone else thought that you would have become, without doubt or regret. Give back to life the best way that you can with what you have in this season of life.

My mom was the epitome of what a woman who pushes through looks like. She unapologetically, but very humbly, pushed past what others thought of her. She pushed beyond the critical voices of public opinion that second-guessed her decision. She pushed past the doubt and fear of "what if." My mom taught me that a life of service was more important that a life of surface success. She pushed past anything that presented itself as a reminder that she should quit and choose the route that was more "logical" or "made more sense." She taught me that having significance was far greater than having stuff. She also taught me that when it comes to living a God-given purpose, not everyone will approve, not everyone will agree and not everyone will "get it." She taught me that in her sweet and quiet spirit, there was such strength, boldness and resilience. She taught me that there is a difference between being impressive and being impactful.

My mom taught me that you don't have to subscribe to the world's philosophy, engage in expectations of how others operate and fit into a pre-existing mold of what success should look like. By example, she taught me that I have the freedom to reject our culture's narrative and create my own success story. Early on, I put a dollar amount on the decisions that my mom made – which I didn't like or understand. Today I am grateful that she chose to live in her God-given purpose, and what she passed on to me is nothing less than priceless. She showed me that when we honor God with our gifts, talents and service, ultimately, the least will become the greatest.

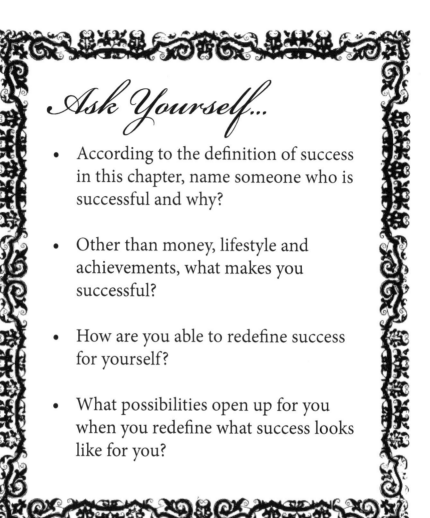

Ask Yourself...

- According to the definition of success in this chapter, name someone who is successful and why?

- Other than money, lifestyle and achievements, what makes you successful?

- How are you able to redefine success for yourself?

- What possibilities open up for you when you redefine what success looks like for you?

"A vision makes you an important link between current reality and the future."

-- Andy Stanley

chapter 8

the 7- step success system

CHAPTER 8:
The 7-Step Success System

I once read a 400-page leadership book, and as informative and enlightening as the content was, the eight words that captivated me the most and became the catalyst for me to pursue my vision was: "A hunter who chases two rabbits misses both."

This resonated with me because I felt I was chasing several visions at once – and was missing them all. I was attempting to have my hands in everything, using my gifts, talents and calling in various areas, but wasn't effective, efficient or impactful in any of them. Because I wasn't clear in my own purpose, my vision was unclear. Without vision, "the people perish," and that's exactly what I was doing. Perishing and far from succeeding, because instead of chasing my purpose, I was too busy chasing multiple "opportunities."

Habakkuk 2:2 reminds us to write the vision and make it plain. However, if we don't clearly know our purpose, how can we write the vision and make it plain? Although we can mentally play around with different thoughts, dreams, and ideas and visually see ourselves doing great things in life, a true vision can't be grasped until we understand and connect with our purpose. In developing our vision, we must be mindful of seven important steps that I created called the I-VISION System:

I – INTENTIONAL

We must decide beforehand what to focus on. The above quote changed my perspective on the importance of being intentional. Being intentional means making strategic and conscious decisions that keep us focused on our vision. Just like a hunter chases two rabbits and misses them both, when we aren't intentional and deliberate with setting priorities, we too will miss out.

If we have multiple areas that we are trying to pursue, we dilute our focus and creative energy, and waste time. In the end, we will probably not achieve our best in any one area. Nothing happens by "accident." Too often, we have several projects and ideas that are all really good and perhaps appear to be something we should take on. But we have to be very diligent with using our time and energy for only those things that support our main vision.

Author Andy Stanley said, "Vision empowers you to move purposefully in a predetermined direction. Without vision, good things will hinder you from achieving the best things." We have to have clarity and discernment about what are "good" things and ideas versus the "best thing" and be mindful and bold enough to forsake all the good things and ideas for what's best.

It doesn't mean that we can't later pick it back up. However, if we allow all the "good things" to be equal to the "best thing," and command the same attention, we'll get sidetracked and never follow through on our vision. It's been said that the good in life is the enemy of the best in life.

V – VISUALIZE

If fear, rejection, self-doubt, time, money, past disappointments and critics were not an issue, what would be possible for you? What becomes available when you focus on the end result of what your dream looks like, instead of all the other distractions that keep us held back and walking into what could be and should be?

To obtain the success that you have defined for yourself, you must first actually be able to see it. Not only do you have to see "it," but you have to see yourself in that success equation. So many times we can visualize success, but it's hard to see ourselves in the picture. As soon as we begin to see ourselves in the picture, we allow sabotaging thoughts to creep in. We remind ourselves why it can't happen, won't happen or shouldn't happen for us.

In essence, we don't think we are worthy of seeing ourselves in the picture of what success looks like. It doesn't become obtainable for us, because we set our gaze on past failures, disappointments and the "what if." Sabotaging and limiting beliefs about ourselves take over and cloud our vision, limiting us on seeing ourselves in the position that we desire to be in.

In order to fulfill the dreams that you have, you must be able to actually see yourself in that role. Mentally rehearse who you want to become and everything you want to accomplish. If you can't see yourself in the role, how will anyone else be able to see you in it? If you're aiming to be a published author, start seeing yourself with your book in hand. Scroll through pictures of yourself and start seeing those pictures on the cover of your book. Visualize yourself at your book launch, signing books and taking pictures with those that have come out to support you. Imagine yourself being interviewed about your book and prepare answers for those questions. Picture yourself at events and conferences selling your books and being excited about the long line before you. See yourself in that role and take a moment to absorb what that experience feels like.

A vision allows you to see what doesn't exist, but yet create the very thing that you imagine. A vision keeps you focused and locked in on what you are seeking to obtain. Without a clear and concise vision, we easily get off track by being seduced in entertaining distractions. Distractions aren't always the "bad" things. A really good opportunity can be a distraction.

The chance to do something interesting and exciting can be a distraction. Offers to join in someone else's great idea can be a distraction. If we aren't intentional, being involved in all the good of life can be a distraction to your overall vision. However, when it comes to your vision, you have to be able to see beyond all those "good" opportunities, so that you can connect with the "best" of them. When we visualize, it allows us to see beyond all the present distractions, lock in on the vision itself and achieve the ultimate goal.

Not only does visualizing keep us focused, it's also our path to the finish line. Again, because of all those "good distractions," it is easy to get sidetracked and make detours. The slightest detour can take us farther than we realize from our vision. That's been one of my biggest challenges — starting something but never finishing it. I could never finish a project, not because I was lazy (well, maybe sometimes) but because I couldn't really visualize what I was working toward.

Again, in theory I could see "it" manifest itself. However, because it was difficult to actually see "me" at the finish line, I could never bring anything to completion. Some of this was self-worth issues coupled with fear. It is difficult to see yourself in a role if you're doubtful that you can fulfill it.

I – Identify your "why"

*Y*our why is the heart of what will ultimately drive you and keep you motivated to continue going forward, even when you don't fully understand the "how" or even the "when." When we have a clear understanding of "why," it gives us the strength and motivation to go forward, even when we want to stop.

Your "why" is critical to accomplish your goals and keeps you inspired. "Why" represents what we believe, our values, what's important to us, and what motivates us. The heart of who you are and what you want to accomplish, is in knowing your "why." You are better able to "sell" yourself when you understand your why. Knowing your why, allows you to better connect with others and allow them to get on board with what you have to offer. Knowing your why allows you to speak the language of your purpose.

If you know your why, it creates an easier path for you to execute. It allows you to make more informed decisions.

Being connected with your why, gives you motivation for your actions. If you don't have a big enough why, you won't take the necessary steps to see "it" to completion. Your "why" is in essence the purpose, reason and cause that inspires you to do what you do. Being clear on your why, provides the momentum to keep going and finish strong, when you physically, emotionally and mentally have tapped out. Your "why" will kick in, take over and do the necessary work when you are mentally and physically too exhausted or disconnected to get things done.

As I was writing this book, I was preparing for my annual women's empowerment event, managing four kids while my husband was often traveling for work and had an editor pushing me to finish another chapter. Not having enough time became a common theme for me. The book project was something very important to me, being tied to my purpose. So since I knew "why," I knew what had to be done. I on many occasions put the kids to bed at 8:00 p.m. and then went immediately to my office and began writing. I continued writing as the sun came up, until it was time to wake the kids and get them ready for school. I dropped them off at school, returned home and continued writing until midday. Although it's not healthy, and definitely not advised, this is an example of your "why" kicking in, taking over and putting in the work, when I didn't think I was capable.

Understanding your "why" makes you better qualified and confident to fulfill your calling. It allows you to do more, to be more inspired and spark change. When you are clear and comfortable with your "why," you are able to detach yourself from the outcome. When we have an expected and anticipated outcome, and our plans don't pan out or go the way we want, this can cause you to abandon your vision or have a defeated spirit. But when we are aligned with our "why", we are able to detach from the outcome of when our plans don't go as expected. Once your "why" is identified, it should fill you with passion and motivate you to keep going. When your "why" is strong enough, it keeps you focused and gives you the ability to execute.

S – Speak it, Start it

When you operate from a place where you are constantly speaking about where you are at, about your current adverse or limiting situation and circumstances, it sabotages your potential and possibility of going to the next level. Constantly speaking on current obstacles and limiting situations leaves you in a stuck, stagnate and draining position.

However, when we speak in a language that places us where we want to be, it is exciting, exhilarating, motivating and empowering. It creates possibility, it presents what could and should be, it awakens those things that are available to us. We were divinely created to have power and authority in the words we speak. Our words have the power to speak life or death into a situation. Words have authority to bring things about and to establish things in our life.

There is a spiritual law that is in operation, whether we know it or not, believe it or not and accept it or not. It is an invisible law. Just like gravity is invisible and whether we can see it, touch it or choose not to believe it, it is present and in operation. Our words have power to affect things in the spiritual realm, which then affects things in the physical realm.

Speak It
Speak the life you seek and not the life you see. The messages

that are sent out from us hold so much power and potency. In order to see our visions manifested, our words have to be in alignment with how we view ourselves down the road. It may seem uncomfortable, or an exaggeration, however, we have to start speaking in terms of "I am," and not "I want to" or "I will one day." We have to start priming our minds to accept and believe the things we are hoping for and believing in. The mind believes everything you tell it. That's one reason so many people are living below their potential or living with limits is because our mind hears, processes and believes the words we say. It doesn't matter what someone else says to you or about you. The only thing that matters is what you say to you about you. Our minds will act accordingly to what it believes and it believes all the things it hears you say.

By speaking it, this is a form of mental rehearsal that positions you to think, speak, act and live as you desire. By doing this, you will have already prepped and primed your mind for your new role. Speak what you seek until your world catches up with your words.

Start It
Of course, we want to be wise and use good judgement in planning and preparing before we start with any new project or idea. We want to make well informed, thought out and wise choices as we spend time on our strategy, plan and execution. However, don't fall into the trap of spending so much time in the planning and strategy phase, that you never actually start on the thing that is in your heart to do.

Too often, we wait for the "right time" to begin and take action on our dreams and decisions. We attempt to wait until all things are aligned just perfectly before we step into it. We waste precious time and drag out the process because we are waiting. We are waiting for more experience, to get it "just right," to finish a course, to become a little more polished, to finish the website, for someone else to make a move first, for someone to notice us and the list continues of excuses and reasons why we "can't" start just yet.

There's a fine line between "speaking it" and the next stage of "starting it." Again, we can find so many reasons to stay in strategy mode, all of which are important and valid. However, at some point, sooner rather than later, even if everything isn't as clear, mapped out and as "perfect" as we would like, we just have to go for it. Just start where you are, in phases, if possible, so that you can evaluate each phase and you don't bite off more than you can chew. We can sabotage everything and get burnt out by trying to execute everything at one time. Start slow and build. There is a world waiting for something that only you can provide and that only you can give. Tackle one area, then add another. But don't wait until all the right elements line up before you start, or you may never begin, or never finish. Sure, where we start will not be where we end up. It won't always start with the bells and whistles or the level that maybe we would like to begin with, and it shouldn't. We will continue to grow and be molded and shaped by our experiences. It's all about jumping in and starting where we're at, and with what we have. We have to remember that as we go along, things will continue to unfold and we will learn and grow as we go.

I – INVESTIGATE

What do you need to get you where you are going? What people do you need to get on board with your idea, to help make it come to life? What research have you done? Who do you need to "sell" yourself and pitch your ideas to? What have you done so far, to get you where you are today? What resources do you have or do you need to help you in your journey of your vision? How do you get from starting point to destination, from conception to completion?

A friend told me something her colleague once said to her as they were embarking on a new project at work: "What's disturbing is that I don't know what I don't know." In other words, there are certain things that she had never encountered before that could have a huge impact on her efforts to be successful, yet she needed to go and learn more about them – whatever it was.

Investigating is ongoing. You have to do your homework. We use this step repeatedly to realize our vision. When you investigate, you are learning from all the resources available to you that can help you find success – webinars, articles, people, experts, mentors, classes, workshops, etc. And what you learn during your ongoing investigation will help you design and refine your road map or plan. Plans can, will and should change. However, the vision stays the same. Your road map is an overall projection, not an actualization, but you need good intel to see your way forward.

O – Obstacles

*I*f we aren't clear in what the obstacles really are, how can we remove them or push beyond them? Obstacles will always present themselves and can thwart our progress. These obstacles can be real, like finances, opportunities and certain people, as well as perceived — like the internal negative chatter that we engage in that keeps us in fear and self-doubt.

We first must identify the obstacles to our success. It was always hard for me to finish things that I had started. I finally had to go through some self-discovery to determine that my biggest obstacle was fear. Along with fear came self-doubt, and insecurity. No wonder I couldn't finish. How could I finish if I was fearful of what would happen, doubtful if I could actually do it, and worried about what others would think?

However, my self-discovery didn't stop there. Once I discovered the "what," I had to dig deeper and figure out the "why" and "where." Why were these obstacles in my life? Where did they come from? Why did they seem to have such a control over me and prevent me from finding fulfillment in my life? After identifying what the obstacles are, we must identify the root of those obstacles.

After much prayer and further exploring, the answer revealed itself to me. I was reminded of the seeds of fear that had been planted from the time I was a little girl and were internalized. I was told: "You can't do that. That's too big. That's not possible. That will never work. You aren't capable. That's for other people. That's a crazy idea. Do something that's safe." So after years of those seeds being planted, then more years of watering and nurturing those seeds, in the end "you reap what you sow." Fear, self-doubt and insecurity were the dominant seeds planted, and as a result, that's what was produced.

Those obstacles were no match for my greater calling and the God-given purpose that I had on my life. I decided to listen to what the promises of God said about my identity instead of the words spoken to me and over me as a young girl. Once I was able to identify what my obstacles were, and then identify the root or source, I was able to push beyond those obstacles in order to fulfill the areas in my life that I desired.

We'll talk more about these obstacles in Chapter 9. I refer to these obstacles as "Sabbies," which is a term I created for the sabotaging and limiting beliefs that we often have about ourselves. These limiting beliefs and mindsets keep us stuck, from walking into our purpose and fulfilling our dreams. However, if we aren't careful of the company we keep and who we allow to enter into our space, we find that toxic people can be one of the biggest obstacles. In the book *Sunday Brunch,* author Dr. Sonique Sailsman says, "sometimes we invite confusion into our own lives by the company we keep or the situations that we choose to get involved with."

As you begin to evaluate the obstacles in your life, consider if the company that you keep is standing in the way of your vision. What becomes available and possible for you if you conquered the obstacles that stand in your way?

N – Non-Negotiables

*I*n order to fulfill our dreams and walk into the vision of our success, we have to put a demand on ourselves, and others. We knowingly or unknowingly make compromises for the sake of convenience, to fit in, to gain the approval of others, to feel better about a decision, to go along with someone else's script or agenda and the list goes on. However, we have to ask ourselves, "What am I not willing to compromise or give up in order to get where I need to be?"

What have you tolerated up to this point? We have to stop tolerating playing small and minimizing our greatness just to make others feel comfortable and at ease about not choosing to elevate and operate in their brilliance. Our top "non-negotiable" is choosing to be unstoppable. When we have a divine vision and God-given purpose that is greater than us, there is nothing that should stop us from answering the call and fulfilling the dream. Not only does our success depend on it, but the success of others as well. The impact and influence of a God-given vision and purpose will outlast us all. Its effects will be experienced and felt well beyond our time. However, success will never come to pass if we continue to negotiate who we are and what we have to offer.

When it's no longer negotiable, our identity, ideas, worth, calling, happiness, vision, success and dreams become unstoppable. When we operate from a space and mindset that commands that notion, we are able to fully show up in the world. You have been given an assignment. The world needs something that only you can provide in the unique manner that you have been designed. In order for you to go forth and fully walk into the destiny that you have been created for and be of service to people that need what only you have to give, you have to no longer be willing to negotiate. Other people have their own script for life. But the creation of your success story must be non-negotiable.

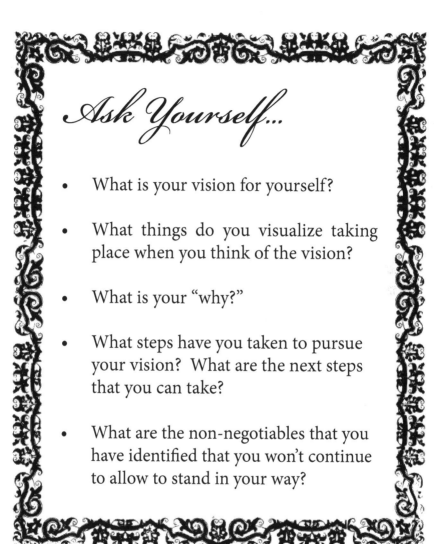

Ask Yourself...

- What is your vision for yourself?

- What things do you visualize taking place when you think of the vision?

- What is your "why?"

- What steps have you taken to pursue your vision? What are the next steps that you can take?

- What are the non-negotiables that you have identified that you won't continue to allow to stand in your way?

*"Remember who you are and make
good decisions."*

Laymen McGrady, age 6

chapter9

who's your sabby?

CHAPTER 9:

Who's Your Sabby?

"I'm not good enough." "I can't do that."
"What will people think?"

hese are words often used when someone is in a self-sabotaging mode. I call these statements or thoughts "Sabbies." What is a Sabby? It's a sabotaging and limiting belief or emotion that we form about ourselves. It is the inner negative and critical self-talk that we rehearse, stopping us from obtaining our dreams. Our Sabbies stem from our inner fears, doubts and insecurities. It's important to recognize these thoughts and beliefs that hold us back and replace them with thoughts of "I can," "I will" and "I must."

At my first "Women Who PUSH" conference, held in Houston, Texas, one of the hallmark activities was "The Sabby Wall." Women wrote down their top three Sabbies on sticky notes and stuck them on the "Sabby Wall." The Sabby Wall is a huge wall that was built to represent the place where women release those self-sabotaging and limiting thoughts that have kept them from moving forward with their dreams and desires.

Once the event was over, I collected all of the notes and reviewed them. I got a little emotional as I began to read the inner most thoughts of women and what held them back from pursuing their dreams or desires. It reminded me of the self-limiting beliefs that once plagued me. The notes were a good sample of what so many women actually feel behind the masks that we wear.

It was a confirmation that the emotional weight women carry is real. It doesn't target the disadvantaged or women who have had their fair share of "bad luck." The conference consisted of business owners, corporate executives and the working women raising a family. There were stay at-home moms, ministry leaders and women who were leaders in their fields. As accomplished as these women were, they were still looking for more. Their Sabbies kept them from experiencing another level of success that they desired in certain areas of their life. On every sticky note there was one common theme in the lives of these women that kept them from living their best – fear.

More than 80 percent of the attendees wrote fear down as their top "Sabby." Again, reading these sticky notes made me realize that as women, we aren't always living up to our full potential and operating in the best version of ourselves. Some level of fear keeps us from claiming what is already ours. This saddened me. As a young girl I was plagued with fear, only to find myself right back in its arms as an adult. I can't say that I am totally in the clear when it comes to having self-limiting thoughts that attempt to creep in and tell me I can't do something. However, I have learned that in order for me to experience the level of success that is for me, I can't allow fear to control me.

Here is a breakdown of the actual Sabbies, in order of the most prevalent:

"I'm not good enough"
"I'm not worth it"
"What will other people think"
"Doubt"
"Fear of rejection"
"Fear of starting"
"Fear of failing"
"I'm not ready/equipped"

All of these thoughts are the result of a conditioned mindset. Although they are innermost thoughts of other women, they have certainly been thoughts that have kept me from moving forward in different areas of my life. I'm a firm believer that everything that we do, or don't do, starts off with a thought. Our mindset is the catalyst for the actions or inactions that we ultimately choose to take. Although we may be in a season of self-limiting thoughts, it's never too late to decide to think differently. Like most things that require a change, it takes some training and time. The same way we trained ourselves to think in a nonproductive way, we have the same ability to train our minds to think in a productive way.

GOLDFISH MINDSET

he one thing that decides and determines who succeeds and who doesn't is our mindset. Our mindset can be our biggest Sabby. What we choose our mindset to be — our attitude and how we view ourselves – will either create and expand our opportunity for success, or it will sabotage and suffocate it.

My kids have chapel once a week at their school and I'm privileged to be one of the speakers to come throughout the school year to share a message with the students. I spoke recently and shared a story with the students about an encounter I had with my own kids and the story of Goldie the goldfish. I was at the pet store not long ago with my kids to restock food for the dogs, frogs, lizard, rabbit and turtle, when they spotted the goldfish display and eagerly campaigned for me to get a goldfish to add to their collection of critters. I told them no and of course they followed with "but why?" One thing was for certain, we didn't need another critter in the house. In that moment I remembered a goldfish story that stuck with me. I responded jokingly: "No, you can't have it because I don't like the way goldfish think."

My kids paused for a moment, looked at me rather puzzled and said, "what do you mean you don't like the way goldfish think?" So when we finally made it back to the car, I told the story of a little girl and her goldfish, Goldie.

One afternoon, a little girl decided to clean out her fishbowl that was quite filthy. She had gone a few weeks beyond the time that she normally cleans the bowl. So instead of putting the fish in the small holding container that she normally used while she cleaned the bowl, she decided to put Goldie in a large oversized tub to give him a little more freedom and room to swim. After she cleaned the bowl, she decided to leave Goldie in the tub a few hours to enjoy his time out of his small fishbowl. She was excited to give him this extra time that she assumed he would use to swim laps up and down the tub and find joy in his new-found freedom.

She came back a few hours later to check on the fish and to put him back in his fishbowl. To her surprise, she didn't find Goldie lapping it up and enjoying life. Instead, Goldie chose to swim in small circles in one corner of the tub.

How many times are we like Goldie? Because of our limiting beliefs and a list of other Sabbies, we remain in a small corner of life. Although we have access to more than we realize, or that we choose to take advantage of, we stay behind the imaginary line for fear of the unknown or what lies ahead. Or perhaps, we see ourselves as just too small to swim beyond the boundaries that we have become accustomed to.

Maybe we think like Goldie, and assume that greater territory that seems so far away, is for "big fish" only. Having a "goldfish mindset" is when we allow the many subconscious, defeating thoughts to keep us behind an imaginary boundary – complacent and circling in our comfort zones. When we don't pursue our highest and best version of ourselves, we never get to experience the fullness and depth of those richer and unchartered waters. A goldfish mindset is any mindset that keeps you from being your best, doing your best, expecting your best, and giving your best. These limiting mindsets inhibit us from embracing our full purpose, power and potential. It limits you from experiencing the fullness, greatness and brilliance of who you are.

What would our society look like today if, as individuals, we didn't step out on faith and into the dark murky waters of the unknown? That's what many women before us had to do to pave the way and change the trajectory of history. You have to trust the God that gave you that vision will also grant you the provision. How many times do we experience having a "goldfish mindset" that sabotages our dreams and vision? Unknowingly, we often choose to live behind the imaginary line, swimming in our small fishbowls of life, instead of moving beyond that line and living life as we were created to do.

Goldie's mindset told him that life in the fishbowl was all he had ever known, and that was the best that was available to him – he believed it. If we aren't careful, we'll believe it too. We'll allow the "Sabbies" in our life, the sabotaging and limiting mindsets, to cut us off from what could be. Lack of confidence, fear, insecurity, doubt and a list of other limiting mindsets will keep us from pursuing our dreams and claiming our destinies.

Our mindset determines how we see ourselves and can send one of two messages. It whispers to us that we are capable of doing something that we want to do; that we're resilient and resourceful enough to bring it all together. It tells us that although it may not be easy, it's possible and that we can do it. On the flip side, our mindset can also tell us the opposite. It can whisper messages that you can't do it and that it's impossible. Our mindset can remind us of the failed attempts and tell us it's going to happen all over again. Our mindset can tell us that we're limited in our abilities and that we need to stick with the smaller things that we can manage and let someone more qualified handle the big, important things.

Our awareness of our mindset is paramount. Our skill set is important, but our mindset is crucial. Mindset is what carries you to the next level and sustains you. It is the one critical foundational element that dictates if you will seize your power or surrender it.

MY OWN PERSONAL SABBIES

*M*y limiting mindset has truly been my biggest Sabby. My Sabbies of fear, insecurity and doubt have kept me swimming in circles in my own little fishbowl, unable to truly pursue my dreams and operate at a higher level. My mindset just wasn't able to "take me there." I would look at women who were around my age, similar educational backgrounds and similar life experiences, and just couldn't figure out how they had it "all together."

In many cases, I actually had more formal education, more life experiences and even more opportunities, but yet they still ran laps around me. How were they able to exude such confidence, walk in their purpose and create their own success, while I was hiding behind a mask and a list of stuff that most would assume success looked like? How could I have pretty much the same background or "better," but yet I wasn't experiencing life on the same level as they were?

Well, after much searching and praying, I found my answer. While we had similar experiences, education and opportunity, the one main ingredient that was missing that we didn't share was the same mindset. You see, where the road split for us was how we saw ourselves and the opportunity that was available to us.

Like I mentioned before, our skill sets were similar. But when it comes to taking action, if you don't have the right mindset, you will never be catapulted into what could and should be. It wasn't until I changed how I viewed myself, and took ownership of my power, that I was able to disconnect with my Sabbies in life and operate out of a mindset of abundance instead of a limited one. I had to start owning my power and stop renting it. We all know the difference between owning something and renting it. When we own something, we view it differently. We take more pride in it. We value it more and have a different level of expectations from ourselves and from others. However, when we rent something, our mindset changes. We don't view it the same. It is temporary and becomes more of a means to an end. We don't have the same level of commitment and we don't typically put in as much care and attention to those things that we rent.

Think about it. Compare the things you have rented in life to the things that you own. When I take a trip and I need to rent a vehicle to drive, sure I take care of it. I do the basic necessary things to get me where I am going, and to return it back in the same condition as I received it. However, I'm not attending to it in the same manner as my own vehicle. I'm not giving it "the works" treatment nor investing in it the way I would my own. This concept is no different than how we see and invest in ourselves. With the correct mindset, we are able to overcome our Sabbies, all of the obstacles, challenges and inner voices that attempt to talk us out of our dreams. We are able to recognize the fear, limits and challenges. The correct mindset will allow us to grow and take control over our fears and not allow the fear to control us.

Speaking of the correct mindset and growth, a couple years ago I read and became enthralled with "Mindset: *The New Psychology of Success.*" In this book, world renowned Stanford University Psychologist Carol Dweck introduced a rather simple idea about how we think. Although simple in theory, it can become quite complex in reality, as we have already discussed. Depending on which of the two mindsets you possess - a fixed or growth mindset- you will either succeed or be stifled in your achievements.

According to Dweck: "In a fixed mindset, people believe their basic qualities, like their intelligence or talent, are simply fixed traits. They spend their time documenting their intelligence or talent instead of developing them. They also believe that talent alone creates success — without effort. They're wrong. In a growth mindset, people believe that their most basic abilities can be developed through dedication and hard work — brains and talent are just the starting point. This view creates a love of learning and a resilience that is essential for great accomplishment. Virtually all great people have had these qualities."

One of my favorite bible passages is Proverbs 23:7 (KJV): "For as he thinketh in his heart, so is he," which, in a nutshell, is the foundation of Dweck's hypothesis.

GET COMFORTABLE WITH THE UNCOMFORTABLE

When I saw that my daughter who plays volleyball, was getting too lax and comfortable with her current level, I had to "help" her make a shift. I had to help shift her by getting her around players who made her a little uncomfortable. Not that the girls on her original team were not hard workers or dominant players, they were. But because my daughter was comfortable, she didn't feel as challenged nor the sense of urgency to push herself further. When you are in the company of people who are strong and dominant in their mindset and skill set, this can create a little intimidation. Although, I knew there was some hesitancy with my daughter playing with a group of girls that made her uncomfortable, I knew that this is what she ultimately needed to boost her confidence and ascend to the next level of performance.

In situations when you are faced with intimidation and feeling a little uncomfortable, it forces you to step up or step down. And for most of us who are seeking to push to the next level of life and possibility, we will choose (eventually) to step up and step out of what is comfortable so that we can enter into the territory of life that stretches us and positions us for something greater. Push beyond your comfort zone. Start to step into the company of those who make you just a little bit uncomfortable.

For years, I surrounded myself with people that made me feel comfortable. They didn't pose a threat to me. They didn't intimidate me. They didn't cause me to look deeper within. They didn't challenge me to be curious about the possibility of "what if." Not saying they were not good people and they weren't seeking better for themselves. By all means they were doing some awesome things. But because we had so many similarities, I was never stretched in my way of thinking.

However, there were other people that I refused to spend too much time with because I felt uncomfortable around them. I felt uncomfortable around them because they represented something that was a bit foreign to me. Perhaps it was their work ethic, their confidence, their skill set and their fierce determination. Maybe the idea that they were just "better" than me in certain areas, was enough to make me avoid them like the plague.

Once I accepted the challenge and began to slowly enter into the presence of a demographic that was different than the group that I took comfort in, something shifted in me. I started to see possibilities. I was inspired in a different way. But most importantly, I saw that I had been wrong all along. They weren't actually better than me like I thought. Instead, they just thought better than me. It reminds me of what one of my favorite authors, Valorie Burton, said in her book *Successful Women Think Differently:* "The edge the successful woman has over the average is in her thought process."

ENLARGE YOUR TERRITORY

My son has a pet turtle and for the past few yearsthe turtle has remained the same small size as he was when we discovered him swimming around in our pool. My son asked me recently "Why hasn't the turtle grown? Why is he still the same exact size?" I explained to him that his turtle grows according to the environment in which he's placed in. Since he's still in the same small aquarium that he first started off in, his growth has been stunted. Enlarging his aquarium would ultimately allow him to grow.

One's environment can have the same effect on people. If we choose to stay in the same 'ole place, around the same 'ole people, we too can stunt our own growth. Stretch yourself, change your mindset and accept the dare to show up in a different way amongst those that make you feel a little uncomfortable. We expand and grow according to our surroundings, so when we stay in our pool of familiarity, we're limited in how far we can go. Enlarge your territory and allow yourself to experience the success that comes from pushing thru those Sabbies.

Ask Yourself...

- When have you had a "goldfish mindset?"

- What are your top three sabbies?

- Do you have a growth mindset or a fixed mindset? Why?

"The most common way people give up their power is by thinking they don't have any."

Alice Walker

chapter 10

from fear to "fear-ce"

CHAPTER 10:
From Fear to "Fear-ce"

Although it was a couple decades ago, I remember it clearly like it was yesterday. Everything about her appearance remains vivid in my head even today – her hairstyle, her dark smoky eyeliner, the small gap between her two front teeth, the way she smacked her lips when she chomped down on her gum, the way she looked me up and down with piercing eyes of disdain, the way she rolled her eyes, the crude and obscene remarks she made to me just for being nearby, the way I would get out of her way and retreat to the other side whenever I saw her coming down the hallways of Philo Middle School.

Her name was Monica Booker and she had me trembling at the knees every time I saw her in school. Perhaps that's why, to this day, I am very sensitive about the topic of bullying. The memories are etched in my mind from my own bully experience, stirring up feelings of anger in me when I hear stories of someone being bullied. On the flip side, I also celebrate when the underdog finally stands up and takes matters into their own hands. On one particular day, I had enough. This was beyond crazy. I was finally over walking in fear every day, wondering if today would be the day Monica Booker finally decided to make good on her word of knocking me out or pulling my hair out. Even more frustrating, I was clueless why she hated me so much. Truth be told, she was probably just as clueless.

On one particular night I decided to go to school with a new attitude. I had mapped it all out in my head. I knew the next day was do or die for me. As long as I was willing to continue to cower down, drop my head, move to the other side of the hall and disregard her obscene slurs and threats towards me, everything would be ok.

But I wasn't willing to be her doormat anymore. I had enough of living in fear. No longer was I going to allow the fear of Monica Booker to get the best of me. It was my 7th grade year for Pete's sake! I had already dealt with her the prior school year and I wasn't going to once again go through another year in terror.

I would go to school the next day, with my head high, and refuse to allow her to continue to disrespect me. But I also had to be clear on what that meant. Not backing down to her could possibly mean I would get knocked out, and I would be coming home with a black eye. This would definitely be the biggest risk I had taken in my 13 years of living. However, I was willing to take the risk. I was willing to be vulnerable. I knew that although she was potentially going to light me up, I knew that I was willing to fight back with all that I had. I knew that if she did get the upper hand on me, I wasn't going to make it easy for her. I was going to look at fear in the face and deal with it.

The next morning came and it was the big day. I usually wore my hair down and wore medium - sized hoop earrings. Not this day. I pulled my hair up in a tight pony tail and ditched the earrings. If today would be the day of battle, I wasn't going to provide my enemy with anything that would give them an advantage over me.

There I was in the sunny school courtyard, minding my business, sitting on a bench, watching some of the kids play four corners. As expected, she, along with her crew, approached me and stood so close to me I probably could have felt her breathing on me, had I not purposely ignored her. I didn't look at her, I didn't budge. I didn't pay her any attention. I continued to look at the other kids who were playing. By this time, the other children noticed that something looked as though it was about to go down, so they stopped playing and talking and cast their undivided attention my way.

I heard Monica Booker clear her throat to get my attention, but I never looked up at her. Usually, by this time, I would have acknowledged her by getting up and moving out of her way. However, I continued to look out into the courtyard, as though I didn't notice her. By this time, a small crowd had gathered around. This was a rare scene: I sat in total disregard of the one who I typically ran from each day. I knew something was about to pop off. I felt the tension, sensed her rage and the whispers and stares amongst the growing crowd made matters even worse.

With sweaty palms and butterflies taking over in my belly, I said a quiet prayer to myself, "Lord, I know I am not supposed to be fighting. I also know I am not supposed to be getting bullied either. So, if I have to fight this girl today, please be on my side. Amen."

Monica Booker finally gave the order and demanded that I move from "her seat." I continued looking out into the courtyard, totally ignoring her as though I didn't hear her. She repeated herself.

This time, without ever giving her eye contact, I nonchalantly responded, "I'm not moving anywhere." She had never heard anything like this coming from me, so she asked me to repeat what I had just said. I looked at her, right dead in her eyes and with a little more bass in my voice, I repeated myself, "I said I'm not getting up and I'm not going anywhere. I was already sitting here."

She was startled by my response. She was under a little pressure because of the crowd of witnesses that had gathered around us. She got even closer to me, in an attempt to intimidate me and yelled, "I said, you better get up before I beat the hell out of you!" Then she proceeded to yell curse words at me too. I still don't know how, but confidence rose up in me. I got bold and told her, "The only thing you are going to do is sit here on the other side of this bench, or you can bring hell on!"

At that point, I stood up, toe to toe with Monica Booker. I didn't know what would happen next, but I was prepared to fight for what was mine — which was my dignity, respect and the right to not walk in fear anymore. I don't quite remember what she said at that point, but I do remember it was no longer me backing down and walking away. This time, after what seemed to be an eternity of a toe-to-toe stare down of who would back away first, she mumbled something, turned around and she and her "posse" walked away.

From that moment on, I didn't have any more problems with Monica Booker. When I walked down the hall, I didn't drop my head and scurry to the other side when I saw her coming. No longer did my stomach get that sour feeling and drop to my feet from her presence. No longer was I scared to use the restroom because of fear of being caught and cornered. Nor did I ever get up to give her my seat again. The fear of Monica Booker no longer controlled me. My entire 6th grade year and half of my 7th grade year had been torture; I could finally exhale. I was "free at last, free at last, thank God almighty, I was free at last!"

Things changed for me on the day I decided to face my greatest fear. It was the catalyst to experiencing a new life that I wanted and deserved, all based on making a single decision. In the previous chapter, we identified fear as being one of women's top "Sabbies" in life. The story of my middle school experience shows that when we stand up to our fears and push through them, we are able to create what we want success to look like.

We often allow everyday fear in our lives to bully us just like Monica Booker bullied me. We cower down to fear, dodge it, allow it to pose a threat to us and dictate our every move. We give our power over to fear and miss out on the opportunities and abundance before us. We scale back our genius and we minimize our greatness, because we bow down to the "Monica Bookers" in our lives. As long as we "bow down," to the fears that bully us around, we don't walk into the fullness of who God created us to be, or our destiny, because we allow fear to rule us.

It is actually our birthright to be fearless and bold, and to thrive in life. We are to live with an expectancy of reaching our fullest and highest potential, but our bullies in life will keep us from experiencing our best if we allow it. What has been your "Monica Booker?" What is it that has bullied you in life? What has been the fear that has kept you from standing up to what you rightfully deserve? Perhaps your "Monica Booker" is fear of not being adequate, fear of what "they" will say or think, fear of not being good enough, fear of not being accepted, fear of your past mistakes, fear to step out and take action, fear of rejection, fear of failure or perhaps, fear of success. I don't know who or what your "Monica Booker" is in your life, but until you finally decide to face your "Monica Bookers", they will continue to control you, dictate and limit you. Like me on that courtyard bench, until we tell our fears, "I'm not moving for you," they will continue to haunt our every step.

We allow the "Monica Bookers" of the world to keep us from walking into our best and creating the life and success that we want. Sometimes success just means looking at fear in the face and saying, "No, not today. Not anymore." When I stood up to Monica Booker, a whole new world of opportunity was opened and created for me. I could finally breathe. I could have a "normal" middle school experience. I could be free to laugh, play and enjoy life without constantly being on the lookout. I experienced a new confidence that I didn't think I had. I became a happier person, I made new friends, and I ditched an enormous amount of stress off of me. In that moment, I went from fear to "fear-ce."

This new life was actually really enjoyable. I had no idea that this was everyone else's "normal." My school experience went to a whole new level, all because I finally told Monica Booker, "No, not anymore."

What world of opportunity will open up and be created for you when you look at fear and say "No, not anymore?" How will you live a fuller life because you aren't busy running from fear? We can get so comfortable in our chaos, and so accustomed to living in fear, that we don't realize there's a whole new world of opportunity. We don't realize that this doesn't have to be our norm.

After years of playing it small, living in a lack versus abundance mindset, living in dysfunction, accepting the status quo, and not fully embracing our brilliance, greatness and power, we conform to those situations and environments as our truth. Our go-to motto becomes "it is what it is." Well, the reality of it is our truth is what we accept and what we create. Our "it is what it is" can be something far greater that exceeds anything that we could imagine or think of.

Until we get to the point where we face all the fears that have bullied us into living a weak, timid and apprehensive life, we will never be able to experience true freedom and take part in a life free from worry and looking over our shoulders. No longer can we allow fear to get in the way of what lies ahead. Too many times we miss out on God's best because our eyes are focused more on the "Monica Bookers" in our life instead of God's promises. Fear will always pop its head up. But how do we handle it? Do we control the fear or does fear control us? It's time for us to make a stand and get ready to fight our fears. It's time that we realize facing some of our fears may be risky and they may put you in a vulnerable situation. However, if nothing changes, nothing will ever change.

At 13 - years - old, my prayer in the school courtyard that day was my way of relying on a greater power than me to get me through. It was really my way of saying, Lord, I may not be able to beat this girl on my own, but with you, I know I will come out of this battle with victory. Although it didn't have to come to a physical match, the outcome was victory. I was successful. I came out in victory because I got everything I needed and wanted, which was for this girl to once and for all, leave me alone.

LESSONS LEARNED

*T*here are always lessons to learn from the things in life that we run from. When we face our fears, the source of our problems may not leave or change, instead we change. Although my fears eventually disappeared, Monica Booker herself didn't disappear (although that wouldn't have been a bad idea). She showed up every day at school, but no longer was I intimidated or afraid. Below are some of those lessons that I learned during this experience, which continue to shape my life today.

Lesson One: Bullies aren't always as big and bad as they appear to be.

Monica Booker had every opportunity to make well on her word and crush me – even more so with an audience watching. Although we have real issues and fears in life, these fears aren't always as big and bad as we make them.

Lesson Two: Until you decide to face your "bullies" or fears, and declare "no more," nothing will change. In fact, the problem and fear only grows.

When I look back on it, who knows how much longer I would have lived in fear of Monica Booker, had I not faced her? It could have dragged on for the remainder of the school year and possibly through to the next year. But the day I said, "no more," was the day that changed everything.

Lesson Three: <u>Sometimes facing your fear means you have to do it scared.</u>

When I went toe to toe with Monica Booker, it wasn't because overnight my fear of her magically disappeared. Not at all. I was sweating bullets and trying to downplay my trembling knees. But I had to face her – scared or not. I wasn't going to let her know that I was scared, but inside it wasn't fun or easy. As a matter of fact, doing it scared is what forced her to back off. Because I did it scared, she saw something different in me. Although I saw a scared, trembling girl, she saw boldness, strength and confidence.

Lesson Four: <u>Change happens when you are willing to be vulnerable and take a risk.</u>

Standing up for myself put me in a very risky and vulnerable position. There was no guarantee that Monica Booker would walk away without a fight. Since I was willing to be vulnerable and take a risk, it turned out as my biggest reward.

Lesson Five: <u>We have a choice to own our power, or give it away.</u>

Once I finally stood up to Monica Booker and she backed away, I experienced freedom for the first time. I was able to relax and enjoy school. I realized that I had a certain inner power. I understood that I had a choice — that I could own my power, or give it away. No longer would I stand powerless.

Lesson Six: <u>Facing your fear produces confidence.</u>

I went from head held low to head held high in what appeared to be overnight. I walked differently, I talked differently and I began to think differently once I faced Monica Booker. I gained a certain level of confidence that I never had before. I realized that this was the confidence that I should have always had, that I could have been experiencing instead of the fear. I also realized that nothing was wasted and nothing was lost. I would not have gained that level of confidence, had I not gone through that experience.

Lesson Seven: <u>Whatever we feed in life, grows.</u>

The more energy and life that we give to our fears, the bigger and real they become. Whatever we water, blossoms. With each passing day, Monica Booker became more of an issue in my life. Even on non-school days, images of Monica Booker swarmed in my head. Even when she wasn't around she was still very present. Once I regained control, there was a shift. I stopped "feeding" her. All of a sudden, what appeared to be a big scary giant, ended up being a little bitty ant.

Lesson Eight: <u>Surrendering to faith, and not fear, opens the door to freedom.</u>

Having faith, believing in something that we don't necessarily see or have proof of, isn't always easy. However, that day in the courtyard, my simple prayer to God, asking for strength to win the battle, showed up big for me. I allowed my faith in believing that I would win—one way or the other—to be bigger than my fear.

FROM A CHILD'S VIEW

Perhaps one of the biggest lessons came from a simple but powerful children's book that I purchased for my kids. My kids and I were at a bookstore when I came across a children's book that piqued my curiosity. It reminds me so much of how our fears and problems can totally take control of our lives and paralyze and immobilize us if we don't face "it."

As simple as the book is, the message is powerful. I'd like to share the book with you.

What Do You Do With A Problem?
By Kobi Yamada

I don't know how it happened,
But one day I had a problem.
I didn't want it, I didn't ask for it.
I really didn't like having a problem, but it was there.

"Why is it here? What does it want?
What do you do with a problem?" I thought.

I wanted to make it go away. I shooed it. I scowled at it. I tried ignoring it. But nothing worked. I started to worry about my problem. What if it swallows me up? What if my problem sneaks up and gets me? What if it takes away all of my things?

I Worried a Lot.

I worried about what would happen. I worried about what could happen. I worried about this and worried about that. And the more I worried, the bigger my problem became. I wished it would just disappear. I tried everything I could to hide from it. I even found ways to disguise myself. But it still found me. And the more I avoided my problem, the more I saw it everywhere. I thought about it all the time. I didn't feel good at all. I couldn't take it anymore. "This has to stop!" I declared. Maybe I was making my problem bigger and scarier that it actually was. After all, my problem hadn't really swallowed me up or attacked me.

I Realized I Had To Face It.

So even though I didn't want to, even though I was really afraid, I got ready and I tackled my problem! When I got face-to-face with it, I discovered something. My problem wasn't what I thought it was. I discovered it had something beautiful inside. My problem held an opportunity! It was an opportunity for me to learn and grow. To be brave. To do something. It showed me that it was important to look closely because some opportunities only come once. So now I see problems differently. I'm not afraid of them anymore, because I know their secret…Every problem has an opportunity for something good. You just have to look for it.

What bully or problem is it time for you to face?

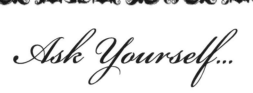

- What role has fear played in your life when it comes to pursuing your dreams?

- How do you handle fear when it shows up in your life?

- Identify a time when although you had fear, you persevered and pushed through the situation.

- If you knew that you would never experience fear, what opportunities would you easily go after?

"You were created to be an original.
Know your worth."

Layla McGrady, age 12

chapter11

answering the call

Chapter 11:
Answering the Call

I was driving home with my 13-year-old daughter from her volleyball practice recently. She was checking one of her social media posts and made a "think out loud" comment. With a disappointed and surprised tone, she blurted out,

"OMG! I didn't really get a lot of likes for this picture." She continued, "Oh well, I'm just gonna have to erase that one."

Intrigued and curious by her comments, I asked her, "Why do you have to erase your picture?"

"Because I only got like four likes for that picture."

I proceeded, "Ok, but why do you have to erase the picture from your account?"

"Because no one really liked it," she said.

"But do you like it?" I asked.

"Yes, I did like it. But now maybe I don't."

"Well what changed about the picture that makes you unsure

if you like it now," I asked. She already knew where I was going with this. I am known amongst my kids for making them think further and for turning everything into a mini lesson. Frustrated, she responded,
"Nothing changed about the picture."
"Of course nothing changed in the picture, Layla," I told her.
"The only thing that changed was you." I continued,
"Layla, as long as you like the picture, that's all that matters. It doesn't matter if no one else likes it or if, for that matter, if everyone likes it. You don't ever change who you are or the path you want to take for the approval of anyone else. Young lady, you are already approved, validated and you don't need the permission of anyone to be who you were created and chosen to be.

DON'T WAIT FOR PERMISSION

*W*e often operate with that same spirit of needing approval and validation and seeking permission from the world to be who we are and go forth in the way that we have been chosen. Just like my daughter, we make decisions based on other's approval or lack of approval. We seek the approval of others and wait on their permission before we see ourselves as worthy or having value. We stunt our success and our potential because we get consumed with what others think, instead of what we think.

A thousand likes won't mean a thing if we don't like ourselves first and foremost. We have to understand and acknowledge not only who we are, but in whose image we have been made. If God not only created us, but He handpicked us, and chose us, then that settles the issue of our identity, worth, and how "likeable" we are. The way I figure it, as long as my Creator "likes" me, His love and approval is all that really matters.

However, the reality is, that isn't all that really matters. We allow our success to depend on how someone else defines it. We wait and take cues from public opinion before we exhale and take ownership. Our success becomes negotiable when we depend on the validation and approval from those around us.

In order for us to be bold and push through, we have to be clear on our identity and assignment. We have to also be clear that others will not always understand that assignment, they won't agree with the assignment and sometimes will be jealous and insecure because of your assignment. Your assignment in life should be non-negotiable. What God gave to you, is for you. He didn't give the vision to everyone else. Therefore, everyone won't understand your mission or see your vision, and won't have access to your provision.

So stop holding back, delaying, second guessing and trading in your dream all because others aren't verbally praising you and affirming you. Their silence doesn't mean that they don't notice you. It often means the opposite: they are watching you.

While you are vexed and bothered because other people aren't responding how you would like them to, rest assured that they are peeking at you from a distance, admiring and wishing that they could be more like you. Some of them just haven't recognized their own potential, power and purpose — and that's okay. By watching you, their admiration of you gives them the strength, boldness and confidence to go forth and fulfill their own dream. Because of what they see in you, it gives them hope.

However, there are "those others." They are also watching, but they're not concerned with their own path to greatness and success. Instead, they are secretly coveting – envious of what you have – because you represent the very thing that they lack. You represent an uncomfortable reminder of their own poor choices, which they choose not to learn from and make improvements. I'm not necessarily referring to the material stuff, but your resilience, which allows you to keep moving even when you've been knocked down; your determination to stay in the game, even when it doesn't make sense; your ability to leap over obstacles and face challenges head on; the favor poured upon you "out of the blue;" the new doors that God opens when the other ones are closed; your decision to declare and claim better days, even in the midst of a battle; your ability to overlook mockery and judgment and push through; your unwavering belief even when the report is negative; your determination to plan for tomorrow when tomorrow has already been denied; your faith in knowing that even without evidence, doors will open.

Lastly, the wisdom that you display and the ability to disregard the foolishness of others and disconnect yourself from needing their approval, all while doing it with a smile, further demonstrates just who you are. Now that's the kind of stuff that they envy. That's the kind of stuff that makes you successful and the very reason that you don't need to seek permission.

Don't shrink the dream, discredit the ideas, minimize the mission, abandon the vision or scale back your genius just to make someone else comfortable. You have too much greatness in you to play it small. You can't afford to downgrade your dreams to fit in with your current reality or to fit in with those around you who choose not to step into their greatness. It is your birthright to walk in the fullness of your destiny.

Just like my daughter was waiting on someone else, when we wait on someone or something else to give us the green light, we hand over our power and hold ourselves back from our greatness. It's as if we've pushed the pause button – placing our dreams on hold.

PLAYING THE WAITING GAME

*T*here have been times in my life when I was on hold from moving forward with something that I wanted to do, all because I was waiting on an outside situation to take place or a person to change before I moved forward. Playing this waiting game, I chose to stay in limbo and not take action. There were times where I waited on my husband to validate me, recognize my value and worth and make certain changes, before I could make certain moves. I was waiting on him to "see me" before I could truly see myself.

I can laugh about it now, but boy how I needed that "permission" from him before I could operate in my own greatness and giftedness and see myself as good enough. I allowed his "lack" of approval, in the way that I thought I needed and wanted, to stop me from doing and being all that I could be. Again, no man or woman should ever have the power to stop you from seeing yourself as already approved, worthy and special. In order to live in the divine flow of who we have been created to be, to experience true success and significance, we have to stop negotiating our value and worth. If God is for you, who can be against you? We create our own success story by not allowing others to stop us in our pursuit of our calling.

You are able to create your own success story when others no longer hold the power to define your worth and value. It's important to be the resourceful and resilient being that you were created to be and not rely on people or circumstances to become your rescue in life. When you cut the rope to the lifesaver that keeps you bound to others approval of who you are and your path in life, you will be able to fully walk in the destiny of your calling and who you were created to be. No man or woman is equipped to be our rescuer. The only source we need to rely on to be our rescue is God the creator.

What do you need to stop waiting on before you take action? Who or what is holding the imaginary key that keeps you from pursuing your dream? It's not always others who we're waiting on. We also wait on our own conditions to be met before we take action. We are busy with "getting ready", which keeps us from executing and actually being ready. We will find ourselves looking up from "getting ready" one day and discover we've missed our opportunity.

Speaking of "getting ready," I love what Oliver Wendell Holmes said about life: "Many people die with their music still in them. Why is this so? Too often it is because they are always getting ready to live. Before they know it, time runs out." Don't allow time to run out for you. I know the many "getting ready "excuses that were personally a challenge for me when it came time to execute. I procrastinated and deferred what was inside of me all because I was waiting and "getting ready."

We get caught up in getting ready, telling ourselves to wait until I get more polished or qualified, when it's the "perfect" timing, when I get a real office, when I get business cards, a website, when I lose a little more weight, when I earn a little more money, when I feel better about myself, and the list goes on. We certainly want to set goals and be wise about when we choose to execute. However, if we aren't careful, we can easily talk ourselves out of those same goals.

QUIET AS IT'S KEPT

*A*re you keeping a dream silent? I have remained silent as a way of protection. However, in the silence, the dreams don't manifest. Our subconscious thought process tells us that we don't have to be accountable for it or explain ourselves if we stay quiet because no one ever knows about it. Our silence provides a scapegoat and an exit plan – an easy way out for us if we need it. Our dreams then become negotiable when we keep them to ourselves. Now I'm certainly not advocating that we need to rally the troops and make a formal public announcement about our intentions. I am a big believer of being mindful of with whom you share your dreams, ideas and visions. Everyone is not going to have the same level of excitement as you. Everyone is not going to "get it," like it or support it—and that's okay, because your dream is for you.

It's equally important to have the right people to tell it to. It is important to surround yourself with other dreamers and doers who are expansive in their thinking and bold in their execution. Who you surround yourself with is who you become. If you are the most successful, the most creative, the most driven, the most intelligent, the biggest dreamer, the most faith-filled in your circle – then it's time to expand your tribe.

THE POWER OF "NO"

*O*nce I worked through my life lessons in owning my identity, connecting with my God given purpose and

About the Author

Author, Life Coach & Inspirational Speaker

CleRenda McGrady finds purpose in making a difference in the lives of women. Audiences leave inspired and enlightened after experiencing CleRenda McGrady, wife of seven-time NBA All-star legend Tracy McGrady and mother of their four children. She is a best-selling author, owner of a coaching business and popular speaker.

A passionate philanthropist, CleRenda uses her financial resources and voice to focus on what matters to her most: encouraging and challenging women to live beyond their inner limitations and motivating girls and teens to believe they are unstoppable. Recognized as one of the "Top 30 Influential Women of Houston," McGrady is a successful entrepreneur and certified life coach. She is inspiring people of all ages to view themselves as full of purpose and capable.

Praise for

Push Thru!

This book is thought provoking, inspiring and definitely a must have tool that can be used by anyone who aspires to birth their vision, dream and fulfill their purpose. What I appreciate most are the questions for self-reflection and the use of personal stories that all can relate to. This is definitely a must read to propel you to the next level of your destiny! I am ready to "push from the right place". - *LaKeisha*

I absolutely love this book. It is informative and inspirational and readers will be able to identify themselves in the book. I just downloaded mine and I am enjoying every page. I recommend it to anyone serious about moving forward. Great message! - *Linda*

This is a great book to inspire those who have been sitting on the bench to get off the bench. An easy and inspirational read! Love the bible verses as well. It made so much sense to connect our purpose with what God wants since He is the creator and made us for a purpose. Thanks for writing this book! - *Anita*

This is a truly inspired work of art. CleRenda has given words to pages and brought them to a step by step plan for successful living with purpose. I literally could not put the book down because each page gave more clarity and confirmation on how I should be "pushing" towards the purpose given to me. There is work for me to do, and I am ready to push. - *Robert*

Man, this is just what the Doctor ordered! Finally a tangible, real, meaningful piece of work that not only gives insight but practical ways that will motivate individuals during their road to SUCESS. May God bless you Mrs. McGrady for your obedience and to the individuals reading, this is what you need to get There!!! Please be prepared to apply what you are reading because application will equal SUCCESS AND FULFILLMENT! - *Amazon Verified Customer*

About Project P.U.S.H.

Project P.U.S.H. is a non-profit organization whose mission is to inspire, ignite and empower teens and women to fulfill their dreams and shift from where they are to where they want to be.

To learn more about CleRenda McGrady's workshops and training courses surrounding the *Push Thru!* concepts and other titles, visit **clerendamcgrady.com.**

To learn more about the non-profit work of Project P.U.S.H., visit **projectpush.org**.

Visit **clerendamcgrady.com** to submit a
speaking request.